LIVING HERE IN ALLENTOWN

BEYOND THE RED DOORS

Second Edition

RED DOOR PUBLICATIONS
Allentown, PA

Red Door Publications is a student organization at Muhlenberg College, in Allentown, PA.

Photos as credited.

Send correspondence to:

Red Door Publications
Muhlenberg College
2400 Chew Street
Allentown, PA 18102

ISBN 978-0-9796268-0-7

Library of Congress Control Number: 2008924749

Printed in the United States of America

Visit *Living Here in Allentown* online

new reviews, discounts,
directions, menus and more

www.theallentownguide.com

ABOUT THIS BOOK

Want some excitement on the weekends? Looking for the perfect gift for that special someone? Sick of the food in GQ? We're here to help. We've assembled a full-proof guide to your new hometown, from its picturesque parks to its celebrated hot dogs.

The book was born out of frustration. Most Muhlenberg students confine themselves to campus. The brave make it as far as the strip malls off Cedar Crest Boulevard, but few of us ever leave the West End. Downtown Allentown may as well be in Jersey.

The guide is meant to change all this—to burst the infamous "Muhlenberg Bubble."

The book was first published in 2005. Two years later, it was clear that the guide needed a face-lift. The 35 seniors in a spring 2007 "Communication and Public Relations" class were the food critics, publicists, editors, and graphic designers who created this second edition. Another team of student publicists, event planners, web designers, and writers helped launch *Living Here* in early 2008. We've added dozens of new restaurants and nightspots, and even moved online (www.theallentownguide.com). It's the best. Guide. Ever. At least until our next edition.

Printing costs were generously covered by Muhlenberg's President's Office, with additional funds from the Office of Admissions. The College's Media and Communication Department deserves special thanks for supporting every facet of the guide's production.

We roamed the city—knocked down pins at the Rose Bowl and indulged in the sinful desserts at the King George Inn—so that you, too, would venture beyond the Red Doors.

PRODUCTION STAFF

SPRING 2007

editorial
MICHAEL IANNACI
LAUREN KRISA
ANDREW PERRELLE
RORY ROSENWALD
LISA WHITE

covers/map
ALLIE O'CONNOR

layout
CRAIG KIND
JANETTE TUCKER

photography
KATIE LINKER
COURTNEY ROOSA

dining
HEATHER ECKMAN
MIKE JOSEPH
KATIE REIMANN
LAUREN TATZ

front of the book
LYDIA HILL
KATIE OLSON

nightlife
STEPHANIE LONGWORTH
LEX MERCADO
LIZ WAICKER

out & about
MEGAN BLESSING
RISA HAMILTON-LIGHTFOOT
LAURA KLENCHESKI

publicity: media
SARAH BURKE
SARAH IVOSEVICH
PAM PHELPS
KARLA AUERMULLER

publisher
RACHAEL DANAHY

senior editorial
MELANIE HEAZEL
JESSICA SALESE
CASEY SANDERS

shopping/resources
RACHEL FRINT
JILL HODGE
CHRIS STRACHAN

treasurer
ANTARCTICA NGUYEN

website
BRIAN AMENDOLAIR

SPRING 2008

advertising
JULIAN LUMPKIN

editorial
SARA HOROWITZ
LAURIE KAMENS
LINDSAY KUTNER

event planning
JAMIE CAPODIFERRO
JENN COLLINS
LEIGH WYNN

publicity
AMANDA GLASSMAN
JENNIFER SHERLOCK
MICHELLE YOST

publisher
BRIANNE SCHUROTT

website
MARISSA CAPUANO
CHRISTIN RAMSEY
JAMIE SCHNEIDER

CONTENTS

MUHLENBERG PICKS

DINING

Allentown Brew Works

Allentown Farmers
Market

Bay Leaf

Bellissimo

Damascus

Federal Grill

La Mexicana Grill

Lo Baido's

Morgan's

Spooners

Sunset Grille

Syb's West End Deli

Tsang's Bistro

Turkish Restaurant

Yocco's

NIGHTLIFE

Allentown Brew Works

Federal Grill

J.P. O'Malley's

Liberty Street Tavern

Rookie's

Stonewall

Stooges

Tally Ho Tavern

OUT & ABOUT

Banana Factory

Cedar Beach Park

Great Allentown Fair

Lehigh Valley IronPigs

Little Lehigh Parkway

Musikfest

BEST OF...

adrenaline rush

Dorney Park's Steel Force Roller Coaster (p. 86)
Riving rafting on the Delaware (p. 85)
Camel Beach at Camelback Mountain (p. 86)
Paintball at Skirmish USA (p. 85)
Hot air balloon ride (p. 86)

great date spots

Bellissimo (p. 11)
La Mexicana Grill (p. 26)
Mangos (p. 28)
Shankweiler's Drive-In (p. 76)
Bravo! (p. 13)

cheers

J.P. O'Malley's (p. 54)
Stooges (p. 60)
Allentown Brew Works (p. 7)
Liberty Street Tavern (p. 55)
Lupo's (p. 55)

chill-out spot

West Park in the spring (p. 79)
Gazebo in the Rose Garden (p. 77)
Pool at J.P. O'Malley's (p. 54)
Bushkill Falls (p. 81)

empty your wallet

Allentown Farmers Market (p. 8)
Edge (p. 17)
Glasbern (p. 19)
Inn of the Falcon (p. 23)
Federal Grill (p. 18)

best bites

Stooges (p. 60)
Chicken Lounge (p. 51)
Parma Pizza (p. 31)
Yocco's (p. 40)
Cali Burrito (p. 15)

culture spots

MusikFest (p. 67)
Civic Theatre (p. 70)
Banana Factory (p. 73)
Allentown Art Museum (p. 69)
Allentown Symphony Orchestra (p. 72)

24/7

Dunkin' Donuts (p. 42)
HamFam (p. 21)
Wegman's
Giant
Gate 7 Diner (p. 18)

family outings

Dorney Park (p. 86)
The Great Allentown Fair (p. 64)
Historic Bethlehem (p. 88)
Jim Thorpe (p. 88)
Allentown Farmers Market (p. 8)

photo ops

Muhlenberg Bell Tower
Canal Park (p. 78)
Jim Thorpe (p. 88)
Rose Garden (p. 77)
Hawk Mountain (p. 82)

LIVING HERE
IN
ALLENTOWN

The Americus building, at Sixth and Hamilton Streets (Philip Johnson)

Allentown, to an outsider, is all Billy Joel lyrics. But when you're *really* living here in Allentown, you forget about the Top 40 caricature. You can't help it, once you've ventured beyond 23rd and Chew.

True, the Allentown we found when *we* left campus has its closed-down factories. The city's riverside Bucky Boyle Park, for instance, sits in the shadow of the abandoned brick-and-copper Neuweiler Brewery—our own Tintern on the Lehigh. From the Eighth Street Bridge, we took in the impossibly vast Mack Truck assembly plant, now idle on the bank of the Little Lehigh. If this is post-industrial decay, it's pretty damn picturesque.

In Joel's "Allentown," it's not just the brick majesty that gets ignored. A couple of blocks up from the Eighth Street Bridge is the Old Allentown historic district. Here we walked along blocks of restored 19th century rowhomes, then stopped in for homemade gelato at Lo Baido's.

Down on Hamilton—the city's main street—we played checkers over fresh soup at Spooners. Back on Hamilton, we were refreshed by the mix of garish awnings and carved-stone facades—none of it market-tested nor climate-controlled. We paused at the fountains in front of the new, glass-and-chrome PPL building, adjacent to its older 22-story Art Deco sibling. We crossed the street to the Allentown Brew Works, where we soaked up the sun in the Biergarten.

Some of the storefronts were empty, it's true. The department stores, including Hess's, were shuttered years ago. A moat of parking lots has cut off nearby, tired-but-resilient neighborhoods.

But we *liked* it on Hamilton—we liked the terra cotta gargoyles on the old Americus Hotel. We liked people-watching at the sidewalk tables of the Federal Grill. We even liked the High Culture Store, martial kitsch and all.

There's no Best Buy on Hamilton Street, nor any other big box parasite. Wal-Mart and the rest—Chi Chi's and the Old Country Buffet included—laze supine along MacArthur Road in nearby Whitehall Township. MacArthur, for all its breath-stealing ugliness, could be anywhere, Phoenix or White Plains. The far West End of Allentown is the same blend of Office Depot and Friendly's.

None of this would matter—the screaming billboards, the half-off signs —if Sleepy's and Petsmart weren't cause to Hamilton Street's effect. There's a larger story here—the gutting of American cities for discount toaster ovens—but for now we're content to appreciate what's left. Forced to choose between MacArthur and Hamilton, we'd take post-industrial "decay" every time.

Well, we're living here in Allentown, at least for the next four years. And we know what Allentown's not.

It's not Williamsburg; they're no cool-hunters nor shock-orange knit caps here, nor even Richard Florida's fabled "creative class." No cool martini bars, no properly dimmed lights. Allentown's not New York; the city often sleeps. It's not Philadelphia, Liberty Bell pride notwithstanding.

Allentown is part Pennsyl-tucky— Yocco's, bowling, gun shows, diners, the 25 *thousand*-seat high school football stadium. There's a lot of Brickote siding and bear-cub flags— and those massive, swaying blown-up

Santas in winter. It's hard to find good Indian food here.

But this cuts both ways: There's no exurban anomie, few professional smiles, no soul-emptying "Oakdale Ridge" developments. No cheesy Tex Mex, no neon signstorm.

In their place we found a *city*. And for all the battering cities have taken, they're still refuges from the market-tested banality of their surroundings. Ours, Allentown, is certainly not the product of any focus group research. Here, Syrian farmers markets hawk Turkish water pipes. You can pick up Dominican, Jamaican, Salvadoran, Cuban and Puerto Rican food within a five-block radius—all for under $5. You drive around this city, and you stumble upon a gorgeous, one thousand acre park. Graceful brick mills sit alongside postcard-worthy blocks of historic rowhomes. Allentown has its share of flag-draped ignorance, to be sure, but also a tough LGBT anti-discrimination ordinance.

We'll take the cramped quarters of La Placita over Don Pablo's any day.

So what are you waiting for? The Red Doors are wide open.

DINING

6 DINING

n the mood for a classy meal? Want some take-out? Don't know where to go? We've scoured the city for you—and stumbled across everything from mom-and-pop Mexican to four-star decadence. Thank God it's not Friday's.

A1 JAPANESE STEAKHOUSE

14 ★★★
$$$$ Japanese
MIN *3300 Lehigh St.*
610-709-0989

No, this Japanese steak house has nothing to do with A1 Steak Sauce, but just like the sauce it is quite yummy. Head past the serene mini-waterfalls and the not-so-serene pink and purple neon to one of five rooms—four for hibachi-style dining and one for sushi. Regardless of what you order, you'll be impressed—and not just by the food (though the fried rice is painfully good). Expect the cook to throw around some knives, do some fun tricks with fire, and even toss some shrimp your way. If you act like a seal, you may just catch a shrimp in your mouth, to the applause of a table full of strangers. What a perfect combination: playing with knives *and* fire. (Open Su-Th 11a-10p; F-Sa 11a-11p.) ☒ ♥

ACI HALAL MEAL & TURKISH RESTAURANT

See TURKISH RESTAURANT

ABRUZZI ON MAIN

25 ★★★
$$$$ Italian
MIN *212 N. Main St., Coopersburg*
610-282-4453
www.abruzzionmainwines.com

Abruzzi on Main might be hard to find since it's located in one of the houses in the sleepy town of Coopersburg.

That look and feel holds inside, too — eating here is like dining in the living room of your home. We found ourselves paralyzed by the news. For appetizers, you can't go wrong with the bruschetta, calamari, or pear salad (all $8). Our top picks for entrees: the filet mignon with a side of pancetta mashed potatoes ($28) and the shrimp with creamy risotto ($24). And be sure to save room for crème brulee for dessert. Abruzzi on Main is serious about wine—they've got an extensive wine list and even offer wine tasting courses on Wednesday nights. Their motto—now our motto—is drink what you like. (Open Tu-F 11:30a-3p, 5p-9:30p; Sa 5p-9:30p.) ☒ ♥

ALADDIN

14 ★★★
$$ Middle Eastern
MIN *651 Union Blvd.*
610-437-4023

Okay, so while it's a little sketchy from the outside, Aladdin is amazing on the inside...jaw-dropping really. The ceiling is low and starry, and the walls are covered in richly colored tapestries. Camel statues line the lower alcoves of the walls, and pillows make the seating extra comfortable. While it's a little pricy, the food is definitely worth every penny. Anyone new to Middle Eastern food should start with the falafel—it's a classic, and especially delicious here. If you plan on drinking, be sure to bring your own, and don't forget to bring an extra $2.50 on Saturdays for the Belly Dancing cover charge. (Open Tu-F 11a-2p, 5p-10p; Sa-Su 5p-10p.) ♦ ♥

ALLENTOWN BREW WORKS

8 ★★★★
$$ Brewpub
MIN *812 W. Hamilton St.*
610-433-7777
www.thebrewworks.com

Paris has its Eiffel Tower. For London, it's St. Paul's Cathedral, while New York boasts the Statue of Liberty. Here in Allentown, we have the Brew Works. We jest, yes, but only slightly: the 400-seat, $7 million brew pub has quickly become, since its 2007 opening, the nerve center of life downtown. One payoff: we no longer need to slog to the Fegley family's original outpost, in Bethlehem (see page 50). The Brew Works occupies four enormous (wide-planked) floors of an old silk factory, and "soaring" seems a feeble description of the steel-beamed ceilings. The food—look out for "beer-enhanced" dishes—is much better than your typical pub fare. We like the pizza special ($9) and the juicy "bacon me bleu" burger ($8.50), though our first love is the mysteriously delicious chicken cheesesteak ($8). And then there are the beers, all brewed on site: five standbys (our favorite is Hop Explosion) and a rotating cast of seasonal offerings (like the high-alcohol Rude Elf Reserve). You could easily get lost here: the ground-floor space, with its underlit bar and glimmering stainless steel brewing tanks, opens onto an outdoor "Biergarten." Downstairs is the "Silk Room," with its L.A. hipster vibe—low-slung black leather couches, votive candles, and a startling two-way mirror (you have to see it). Take the wide staircase to the second floor "High Gravity" bar and dining area, which hosts live music on the weekends and comedy on Tuesday nights. Thursday is "College Pub Night," so bring your Muhlenberg ID for specials. And don't forget to leave with a "growler" ($3, $8 to fill) of craft brew. (Open daily 11a-2a.) ♪ ♼ ⚮

LEGEND

🐷 MUHLENBERG PICK	MINUTES FROM CAMPUS, BY CAR	**8**
$ LESS THAN $10 PER MEAL	BETWEEN $15 & $20 PER MEAL	**$$$**
$$ BETWEEN $10 & $15 PER MEAL	OVER $20 PER MEAL	**$$$$**
♼ ALCOHOL SERVED	DELIVERY	🏃
BRING YOUR OWN	LIVE MUSIC	♪
💰 CASH ONLY	TAKEOUT	🥡
♥ DATEWORTHY	OUTDOOR SEATING	⚮

DINING

8 DINING

DINING

ALLENTOWN FARMERS MARKET

2 MIN
★★★★
$-$$ Everything
Allentown Fairgrounds
610-432-8425
www.fairgroundfarmersmkt.com

Have you ever wanted to travel around the world in 30 minutes? Three days each week (Thursdays, Fridays and Saturdays), the Allentown Fairgrounds hosts the legendary Farmers Market, a mini version of Philadelphia's Reading Terminal Market. The self-proclaimed "most modern old-fashioned-style market in the East," the Farmers Market is condensed Allentown goodness. The sixty-plus vendors who set up temporary shop here cover all the food groups and then some—there's pizza, Chinese and Mediterranean food, amazing BBQ chicken and ribs, pies and pastries, deli meats and fresh breads, cheeses, fresh fruits and vegetables. As if that weren't enough, there are also candles, flowers, gifts, wine and an on-site flea market. Prepare for sensory overload: hand-painted Amish farm signs compete for space with down-home murals and Allentown's elderly. Ninety-thousand square feet never felt so small. We thought we'd take you on a brief (and selective) tour, starting at the market's far west end. As you enter, you can't miss **Charlie K's Pizza**, great for takeout but also your source for bake-your-own pies. Around the corner, you'll find **Ribs N' Things,** where the soup-genius cook prepares over 60 varieties each week for $5-$6 (try the Jambalaya). Walk past **Pearl's Smoke Shop** to **Danny D and Denise's Fairgrounds Luncheonette**, for delicious cheesesteaks and burgers, Buy a few dozen kiffles (PA Dutch pastries) at the **Kiffle Kitchen Bakery,** and drop in for some local wine at the **Clover Hill Winery** store. Head back past the Luncheonette, turn right, and behold the truly startling variety of hormone-free sausage and poultry at the **Mr. Bill's.** On your right, you'll pass fried fish at **Bobby Mo's,** Italian specialties at **Uncle Angelio's** (try the fresh-baked calzones), and prepared Mexican dishes at the **Sweets Grill.** Don't be intimidated by the cheese selection at **Wittman's World Cheeses**, on your left, but do try a barrel-drawn pickle from **New York Pickle**, on your right. Just a bit further along, **Mink's Candies** is a dentist's nightmare, across from **Berghold's Produce**, with the freshest, greenest produce in Allentown. (They supply most of our fine dining establishments.) Down the

Allentown Farmers Market, at the Fairgrounds (Philip Johnson)

ramp, fight the crowds at **Dan's Bar-B-Que**, where you must stop, sit, and consume BBQ chicken and cornbread. Turn right, and around the corner you'll find **Southern Delights**, our favorite spot for blacked eyed peas and collard greens. As you continue east, be sure to try the crab cakes at **Atlantic Oyster Co.** Across from Atlantic are the Valley's best donuts, from **Mary Ann Donut Kitchen**. Don't tire yet! Further east is **Fan's Asian Flavors**, with delicious sushi, which is across from Allentown's gyro heaven, **Foods of the Mediterranean.** Miss your mother's pierogis? Try **Gdynia Polish Market**, just beyond Fan's. What are you waiting for? Get off your ass and walk somewhere for once! (Open Th 9a-8p; F 8a-8p; Sa 8a-6p.) 🌱

AMAZON CAFE

8 ★★
MIN $ Cafe
835 Hamilton St.
610-776-1717
www.amazoncafe.com

The Amazon Café calls itself a healthy alternative to fast food. It's certainly more figure-friendly than next-door neighbor Johnny Mañanas. The menu, along with a giant toucan mascot, includes nutritious soups, paninis, wraps, salads, and pastries. But it's their delicious signature smoothies—like Paradise Lust, the Coldblaster, and Bananarama—that make the drive downtown worthwhile. Keep in mind that the Amazon Café is pretty cramped—it's only got a counter with some stools, a pair of tables, and a couch—so take your smoothie to the fountain-filled plaza outside. Be warned that resistance to a fountain drenching is, in fact, futile. (Open M-F 7a-4p.) 🌱

AMIGO MIO

11 ★★★
MIN $$$ Mexican
545 Cleveland St.
610-776-2026

If this is your first time, you probably just passed Amigo Mio. Turn the car around, and drive more slowly this time! Yes, it's in a plain row house, and no, there isn't a parking lot. But trust us: it's worth it. The Mexican here is tasty and there's nothing remotely Tex about it. You'll be seated in Amigo's single, living-room sized dining area, and surprised to find a full bar and warm yellow walls. All entrees are reasonably priced at $3 to $4 but surprisingly small, so don't be afraid to order two. If your satisfied stomach is brave enough to take on dessert, try the flan. This is no ordinary flan—it comes in flavors like double chocolate and pumpkin. So fire up your GPS and remember to bring cash. (Open W-F 5p-9p.) 🔥 ♥ 🍸

APOLLO GRILL

21 ★★★★
MIN $$$ Trad'l American
85 W. Broad St., Bethlehem
610-865-9600
www.apollogrill.com

It's really your pick when it comes to a night out at the Apollo Grill. The place is a combination of fancy restaurant and sports bar; a dimly lit, slightly overcrowded dining area full of beautiful paintings adjacent to a bar with a television screen for ESPN. The food, wherever you end up, is delicious. Like the crowd and atmosphere, the menu is split between affordable fare and items to save for a night when you're planning to step up to your "A-game." While entrees typically run $11 to $25, there's plenty to fit the college budget: the appetizers, club sandwiches, burgers, pizzas, and pastas are all priced from $7 to $11. For the older crowd, there's a dizzying array of martinis and wines. Beware the dessert menu you'll get before receiving your bill—it's hard to resist. The Apollo Grill is nice but not over the top—the perfect place to take first dates, long-time loves, and parents. (Open Tu-Sa 11a-10p.) ♥ ♈

AWILDA'S

10 ★★
$ Dominican
MIN *546 N. 7th St.*
610-770-0661

Allentown is a burgeoning center of Latin American cuisine. Allentown? Yes, and Awilda's is the newest reason to venture downtown for cheap, delicious Latin fare. The Dominican newcomer sits in a stately 19th-century row house, the former home of the Century Cafe. This means that you get to savor your fried green plantains ($2) in wood-paneled, stained-glass elegance. Take an old wood booth, or sit along the walnut, wrap-around bar (but bring your own beer). Awilda's portions sprawl across the plate, and each dish gets served with steaming piles of rice and beans—for the price of a Happy Meal. The beef stew ($4.50) comes in tender, delicious shreds; try it with a beef-stuffed sweet plantain ($3). We're told that the goat ($6) and oxtail ($6) stews are especially tasty. We'll take their words for it. (Open daily 8a-1a.) 🥡 🍶

BACIO

8 ★★★
$$$$ Italian
MIN *1259 S. Cedar Crest Blvd.*
610-821-1102
www.bacio-restaurant.com

After you're seated deep within the bricked grotto, you'll forgive Bacio for its office park setting. Shadow-boxed candles line sections of the wall, while music from crooners like Frank Sinatra and Andrea Bocelli plays in the background. Obsess over the menu while enjoying a complimentary serving of bruschetta and fresh mozzarella with tomatoes. Bacio's entrees range from traditional dishes like gnocchi to less conventional fare, like the incrostato filleto di manzo (grilled beef tenderloin with gorgonzola topping and chianti-pecorino sauce, $24). Popular pasta choices include the ravioli di manzo (ravioli with meat, $14), and the ravioli dolce creama (ravioli stuffed with shrimp, crabmeat, spinach and ricotta). Serving sizes are generous (you can always opt for a half portion at half price) but leave room for dessert—the tiramisu or triple layer chocolate and peanut butter cake are too tempting to pass up. Our only advice: wear an adjustable belt. (Open M-Th 11a-10p; F 11a-11p; Sa 5p-10p.) ♥ ♈

BALASIA

15 ★★★★
$$ Vegetarian
MIN *500 Chestnut St., Emmaus*
484-330-6405
www.balasia.net

Mere vegetarians are such wussies! At Balasia, vegans run the show, and even the carnivores among us are grateful. Balasia is set in a fabulous Victorian mansion in nearby Emmaus, though the homemade dishes are even more beautiful—a kaleidoscope of fresh and artfully arranged vegetables. The vibe is earthy, with bamboo placemats and scented acorns at every table. Your host is also the owner and cook, and she'll happily recount her travels through India, studies of botany, and 11-year commitment to vegan foods. Her menu changes every day and the drink specials are all organic (including everything from red peach soda to Kombucha, a Himalayan tonic). Make

The Bay Leaf Restaurant, on Hamilton Street (Sara Rosoff)

sure you try the Peanut Butter Bombe, so rich that you would never know it isn't chocolate. Down with the lactose-industrial complex! (Open Tu-W 11a-4p; Th-F 11a-4p, 5p-11p, Sa 5p-11p.) ♥

THE BAY LEAF

8 ★★★★
$$$$ Asian Fusion
MIN *935 Hamilton St.*
610-433-4211
www.allentownbayleaf.com

While there are cheaper options for a tasty meal, it's definitely worth forking out a couple extra bucks for the Bay Leaf. The decor looks more like an airport lounge than a fine restaurant, but the food more than makes up for it. Begin with any of the reasonably priced starters or salads, such as the inventive Mango Napoleon, which combines a tropical salad with crab meat. Entrees range from Thai-inspired creations to seafood and veal dishes, which are all equally delectable. The Bay Leaf proves that culinary

excellence can be found without leaving downtown Allentown. (Open M-F 11:30a-2p, 5p-10p; Sa 5p-10p.) ♥

BELLISSIMO

5 ★★★★
$$$ Italian
MIN *1243 Tilghman St.*
610-770-7717

On one of the busiest streets in Allentown lies a quaint garden courtyard, filled with Roman statues and fountains. At Bellissimo, you reward your senses long before the food's brought out. (Inside, too: The dimly lit, tiled dining room is a long way from the chaos of Seeger's.) Each meal begins with Italian rolls dipped in hot garlic and oil. Don't skip the appetizers here: The hot antipasto, with Italian meats, cheeses and fish, is particularly good. The entrees are generously portioned, and rarely disappointing. Tuscan wine, elegant music, the soft gurgle of a fountain: it's easy to forget—and depressing to remember—that you're a few car lots

Bellissimo, at 13th and Tilghman Streets (Rachael Danahy)

away from campus. (Open Tu-Su 11a-10p.) ♥ 🍸 🍸

BETHLEHEM BREW WORKS

See NIGHTLIFE

BILLY'S DOWNTOWN DINER

17 ★★
$ Diner
MIN *10 E. Broad St., Bethlehem*
610-867-0105
www.billysdiner.com

Billy's Downtown Diner is diner grub taken to the next level. Located in the heart of historic Bethlehem, Billy's is a place where they might not know your name, but Billy himself may very well greet and seat you. The menu has an eclectic mix of dishes all under $10. Our favorites are the omelets, served with home fries and toast and priced around $5. This isn't, sadly, the place

to get breakfast for dinner—Billy's closes at 4pm on weekdays and 3pm on weekends. (Open M-F 7a-4p; Sa-Su 7a-3p.)

BLACK ORCHID

8 ★★★
$$$ Southern
MIN *1207 N. 12th St.*
484-664-7733

Living by the motto, "we cook what we want to eat," the chef at Black Orchid serves up a smorgasbord of fusion food that's hard to pigeonhole. While the no-frills exterior and floor-to-ceiling mauve walls inside might not excite the senses, the food comes to the rescue. With colorful appetizers like collard green dip, served with warm, homemade tortilla chips, and soul food-inspired entrees like tamarind baby back ribs and Creole shrimp, everything on the menu is full of vibrant spice and flavor. The portions start out big, but each dish also comes with a choice of two sides. We recommend the collard greens, corn pudding, and especially the candied yams. Even the macaroni and cheese is a creamy delight. No matter what you order, make sure to wash down your meal with a sweat tea—theirs is spectacular. Regardless of what you're in the mood for—Southern or Caribbean-inspired, even Italian—the chef at Black Orchid is ready to prepare it from scratch. Just plan on a wait—home-cooked meals take time! (Open Tu-Su 11a-2p, 5p-9p.) 🍽 🍸 🍴

THE BRASS RAIL

12 ★★★
$$ Italian
MIN *3015 Lehigh St.*
610-797-1927
www.brassrailrestaurant.com

The Brass Rail has put the "f" in family restaurant since 1917, when it opened as a hotdog and hamburger stand in downtown Allentown. Technically an Italian restaurant, the Rail serves something for everyone: pasta dishes, fish, steak, burgers, pizza, famous cheesesteaks (hailed as the best in the city) and drinks (check out the specials). Though very diner-esque, with the large menu, low prices, and cash register up front, it has a far more homey feel: a fireplace with fake logs burning, paper holiday decorations—the exact ones you swear your Mom puts up at home—and a waiting room full of small children and old ladies with walkers. We certainly endorse the Brass's motto (proudly displayed on a variety of merchandise): "Get off your brass and come to the rail!" Oh, and don't be surprised if you hear the place break into a rousing rendition of "Happy Birthday to Grandma!"—trust us, it's bound to happen. (Open M-Th 7a-midnight; F-Sa 7a-1a; Su 8a-10p.) 🍸

BRAVO!

11 ★★★
$$$$ Italian
MIN *Lehigh Valley Mall, Whitehall*
610-266-4050
www.bravoitalian.com

The dark, romantic lighting and open-spaced interior is a perfect complement to Bravo's unique, wide-ranging menu. While offering traditional items like eggplant parmesan and spaghetti Bolognese, most of the dishes are spiced up with a little something extra, like orzotto with mushrooms and prosciutto and the variety of flatbread pizzas. Even a simple dish like the balsamic marinated chicken is fresh-tasting, with the addition of cooked vegetables and a light balsamic dressing. The olive oil that accompanies the traditional break basket is flavorful, with a touch of spice and ginger-inspired sauce. The extensive wine and cocktail menu adds to the classy atmosphere at this popular Shops at Lehigh Valley Mall restaurant. On the weekends, the ever-so-long wait for a table is quickly forgotten, thanks to the friendly and attractive waitstaff. The rustic, dark wood area at the bar is a relaxing place to wait with a drink. We say: Bravo! (Open Su-Th 11a-10p; F-Sa 11a-11p.) 🍸 ♥ 🍴

BUCA DI BEPPO

15 ★★★
$$$ Italian
MIN *714 Grape St., Whitehall*
610-264-3389
www.bucadibeppo.com

With its gaudy, gold-framed photographs, its large, color-bulbed Christmas lights and oversized plastic cakes on the walls, this deliciously kitschy Italian restaurant is so tacky it's fun. There is a Pope Room, complete with a bust of the pontiff in the middle

DINING

of a round table, and music playing overhead from great Italian-American singers like Frank Sinatra and Dean Martin. The bathrooms take the experience to the next level: You'll find pictures of naked people, and hear the opposite sex speaking Italian over the stereo system. For dates? Not so much. But Buca is perfect for large groups, because the dishes are served to be shared, family-style, right down to the desserts. When you're being seated, you're led through the kitchen and greeted by everyone—even the chef. Check your diet at the door, as the food here is high-calorie and high-carb, but every bite is worth it. You can't screw up your order, but the macaroni rosa and chicken parmigiana are favorites. If, by some miracle, you have room, the bella festa is a cake-and-ice-cream masterpiece. (Open M-Th 11a-10p; F-Sa 11a-11p; Su 11a-9p.) Ɏ

BUCKEYE TAVERN
18 ★★ $$$ Steakhouse
MIN 3741 Brookside Rd., Macungie
610-966-4411
www.buckeyetavern.com

Got extra cash to burn or parents in town? Try the Buckeye. Dishes range from the mundane (like nachos) to the classy (like the crabmeat Colorado, a $30 dish featuring filet mignon and lump crab meat). Set in a stone tavern from the 1700s, the decor is a little tacky—think Cracker Barrel on steroids. While service is inconsistent, appetizers like the cheesy garlic bread more than make up for it. (Open M-F 11a-9p; Sa noon-10p; Su noon-9p.) Ɏ

CACTUS BLUE
18 ★★★ $$ Mexican
MIN 2915 Schoenersville Rd., Bethlehem
610-814-3000
www.cactusblue.biz

Cactus Blue is one hot tamale. Voted best Mexican food in the Lehigh Valley in 2005 and 2006, this hole-in-the-wall more than earned the accolades. The service is outstanding, the food is delicious and fresh, and the colorful decor and atmosphere round out the experience. Complement a flavorful dish—we'd suggest the enchiladas or chimichangas with beef so tender you won't even need a knife—with a refreshing Mexican mango soda. And end your meal with a bang thanks to Cactus Blue's banana cream-filled churros. When you go (and you must!), don't forget to arrive early or make a reservation because the cantina fills up quick. (Open M-Th 11a-9p; F-Sa 11a-10p.) ♥ 🍶 🗑

THE CAFÉ
17 ★★★ $$$$ Thai
MIN 221 W. Broad St., Bethlehem
610-866-1686

Tucked away in a beautiful two-story, Victorian home, the Café can easily be missed in your quest for that romantic date-spot. Now you've got no excuse! The Café's elegant, yet homey decor provides a lovely backdrop for any meal. Thanks to both American and Thai chefs, its kitchen cooks up a unique range of generously portioned lunch and dinner items. If your palate enjoys a spicy kick, the Café will not disappoint. Don't skip the appetizers here: the chicken satay, spring rolls, and spicy soups are out of this world. Most dishes, like rack of lamb, filet mignon, and salmon, can be served in either an American or Thai style. The menu also features strictly Thai dishes such as delicious shrimp pad Thai, and chicken curry. You will definitely want to leave room for the frightfully tasty homemade desserts. At the end of the meal, the pleasant and knowledgeable wait staff will show you into a smaller room that acts as a pastry shop. Here you can choose from an array of cookies, cakes, pies, and tarts. (Open Tu-F 11a-2p, 5p-8:30p; Sa 5p-9:30p.) ♥ ⍦

CAFE BUON GUSTO
4 ★★
$$$ Italian
MIN *1901 Hamilton St.*
610-782-0900

Here's good Italian food without pretension. Café Buon Gusto is half pizzeria and half dining room, so feel free to call ahead and order from the take-out menu, or enjoy a sit-down dinner. Either way, you won't be disappointed. Their entrees (around $17) include pasta, veal, chicken, seafood, and steak dishes, and are served with bread, salad, and a choice of pasta. The pollo parmigiana is tasty, though we found the pollo francese a little too lemony. Prepare for large servings and save trunk space for leftovers. And don't forget to bring your own bottle of vino. (Open M-Sa 11a-10p; Su 4p-10p.) ♥ 🍶

CALI BURRITO
3 ★★★
$ Mexican
MIN *3104 Hamilton Blvd.*
610-351-1971
www.caliburrito.com

The quintessential surfer food must have gotten lost on the way to the Jersey Shore, because it has nestled itself at Cali Burrito, here in the Valley. Offering multiple variations of San Francisco-style burritos and tacos, Cali Burrito is that rare fast food place that uses fresh ingredients and vegetarian options. The prices are student-appropriate, though the waves—they're still two hours away. (Open M-Sa 11a-9p; Su 11a-3p.) 🥡

CARIBBEAN DELIGHT
10 ★★
$ Jamaican
MIN *465 Washington St.*
610-770-9832

There's south, and then there's *south.* The friendly chefs at Caribbean Delight fry up soul food and Jamaican fare—so you can get your curry goat ($7) with a side of collard greens ($2). The xeroxed menu divides straight down the middle, but it's all cheap. Frightfully cheap, actually: the delicious jerk chicken dinner is only $8, and comes with salad and a steaming pile of rice and peas. Soul food, too: With the fried chicken platter ($8)—greasy and proud—you get two sides (yams, for example, or mac & cheese) and cornbread. The place is definitely dress-down (when in Jamaica...), festooned with kitschy island decor. Tissue-paper palm trees crowd the ship-style wood panelling, as a giant, smiling Bob Marley mural overlooks the modest, plastic-topped tables. It's not spring break exactly, but it's as close as you'll get in Allentown. (Open M-W 11a-9p; Th-F 11a-11p; Sa noon-11p; Su 1p-9p.) 🍶 🍶

16 DINING

DINING

CARRABBA'S ITALIAN GRILL

5 ★★★
$$ Italian
MIN *510 S. Cedar Crest Blvd.*
610-439-6100
www.carrabbas.com

As any good Sicilian knows, a meal is better when it's made with a family recipe, lots of garlic and a touch of love. Carrabba's founders used just that philosophy when they first set up shop in Houston. They're regularly packing 'em into the Allentown outlet, a low-lit, comfortable space with Frank Sinatra singing in the background. Appetizers like the crab cakes, seared in a cast iron skillet and served with a roasted bell pepper sauce, will leave you begging for more. You'll need a healthy appetite to finish one of the main courses, but irresistible choices like the lobster ravioli served in a white wine cream sauce or the pollo rosa maria chicken, stuffed with fontina cheese and prosciutto, are worth the "need to nap in the car before driving home" feeling of fullness and satisfaction. (Open M-Th 4p-10p; F 4p-11p; Sa 3p-11p; Su 2p-9:30p.) ♥ ⏉

CHARLIE BROWN'S

7 ★★★
$$$ Steakhouse
MIN *1908 Walbert Ave.*
610-437-1070
www.charliebrowns.com

Is your inner carnivore screaming for steak? For some of the best in Allentown, saddle up and head out to Charlie Brown's Steakhouse—part of the New Jersey-based chain. Prime rib's their specialty, but they also dish out chicken, seafood, and tasty burgers. (Vegetarians, you're limited to ravioli and a plentiful salad bar.) Drink specials include $1.50 margaritas on Tuesdays and $2 pints on Thursdays. The space is almost as delectable as

the meat—special rooms for larger parties, a bar and lounge area and a cozy fireplace. The main drawback are the crowds at this popular spot, so be sure to reserve a table in advance. (Open M-Sa 11:30a-10p.) ⏉ ♥

CHICKEN LOUNGE
See NIGHTLIFE

A CUP & SUCH GOURMET COFFEE SHOP
See SPOONERS

DAMASCUS

7 ★★★★
$ Middle Eastern
MIN *449 N. 2nd St.*
610-432-2036

Sensational shwarma, mouthwatering hummus and don't even get us started on the fried eggplant... While the decor's a bit spare at this family operation, they've got some of the best Middle Eastern food in the area—a huge variety of Syrian specialties, including plenty of vegetarian options. (They also serve a few more conventional dishes—like chicken sandwiches and burgers—for less adventurous eaters.) Since entrees average $8 and pitas less than $4, you won't have to spend a fortune to get a truly fantastic meal. (Open M-Sa 9a-9p.) 🍶 🍱

DOGSTARR CAFE

10 ★★★
$ Cafe
MIN *29 N. 6th St.*
610-821-1011

For those groggy, slightly hungover mornings when the last thing you want to do is see someone you know, the DogStarr Cafe provides quality food with a side of guaranteed privacy. Adjacent to the Allentown Symphony Hall, the cafe has been serving local business people for over ten years. It's got an exceptional (and reasonably priced) menu of breakfast and lunch items, from bagels to salads and sandwiches. And who needs a mainstream Starbucks when the funkier Dogstarr has everything a coffee- or tea-lover could wish for? You'll be pleasantly surprised by the list of lattes and cappuccinos, flavored coffees and Chai and regular teas. And no one will judge you for your sweats. (Open M-F 8a-4:30p.) 🖐

DUNDERBAK'S

10 ★★
$$ German
MIN *121 Lehigh Valley Mall, Whitehall*
610-264-4963
www.dunderbak.com

Attention hungry shoppers: Just beyond Macy's perfume counter in the Lehigh Valley Mall awaits the smell of …*sauerkraut*? For the most part, Allentown seems to have forgotten its rich German heritage where dining is concerned. Dunderbak's is one of the very few exceptions. It's often overlooked since it's one of many options at the mall, and the dining area itself is hidden behind a gift shop (where you can choose between ten different kinds of sauerkraut) and quick-service counter (great for a sausage on the go). Your first impression once you wander back: beer. It's responsible for most of the interior decorating—it lines the walls on shelves and in coolers—and for filling out a very lengthy drink list. (Just try to name their more than 200 varieties.) Whether you're drinking or not, try the food for a real taste of *Deutschland*. Try the griebenschmalz or dogs with wurst, or their signature grilled reuben. The service is quick but don't look to the servers for much

additional assistance. While it isn't stellar, Dunderbak's is a great reason to skip the food court during your next trip to the mall. (Open during mall hours.) ¥

EDGE

18 ★★★★
$$$$ Asian Fusion
MIN *74 W. Broad St., Bethlehem*
610-814-0100
www.edgerestaurant.net

Flawless food, graceful service and a modish air. If that's what you're looking for—and if you're willing to leave Allentown—then Edge is your place. Edge, in historic downtown Bethlehem, bills itself as a dash of New York in Pennsylvania, and we can see why. Start your cosmopolitan evening with, well, a cosmo, as the bar mixes some of the best. Not 21? You can still dine Manhattan-style. Start with the prosciutto San Danielle ($10) or the baby field greens with toasted walnuts, Roquefort cheese, and a roasted shallot vinaigrette ($9). For your main course, we suggest the New York strip steak ($30 and just what you'd expect from Luger's) or the handmade cavatelli with rock shrimp ($22). And the Normandy apple tart and Valrhona chocolate cake (both $9) are some of the best desserts you'll find this side of the Lincoln Tunnel. So hail a cab and enjoy big city dining right here in the Valley. (Open M-Th 5p-10p; F-Sa 5p-11p.) ¥ ♥

EL CASTILLO DEL CARIBE

11 ★★★
$$ Dominican
MIN *346 Ridge Ave.*
610-776-0914

El Castillo is unique, to say the least. Its mix of a hectic take-out business and casual, bright-lit dining makes for a bizarre ambiance, though the service

18 DINING

is friendly and welcoming. The dining room is small, but the portions large. If you stop by El Castillo only once, order the paella ($15)—you will thank us. Some of the seafood can be pricey; seafood soupy rice is $23, and the mashed fried green plantains with octopus is $12. Meat dishes, on the other hand, are inexpensive; the mashed fried green plantains with chicken is $4, and the BBQ pork ribs is $5. If you're looking for lighter fare, the lettuce, tomato and avocado salad ($3.50) is tasty as an appetizer or a meal. These Dominican dishes are full of flavor and color and definitely worth a try. (Open daily 7a-11p.) 🍴 🍷 🏃

FARMERS MARKET

See ALLENTOWN FARMERS MARKET

THE FARMHOUSE

16 ★★★
$$$$ Continental
MIN *1449 Chestnut St., Emmaus*
610-976-6225
www.thefarmhouse.com

With its proper staff, limited entrees, and high prices, the Farmhouse is striving for (accent please) f-i-n-e d-i-n-i-n-g. We found the atmosphere a bit stuffy and better suited for the AARP crowd. The real find is the Farmhouse's downstairs bar. The space feels like an old wine cellar, with dim lighting and rustic stone walls. It's got a romantic, almost mysterious vibe, along with a wide array of beers, wines, and spirits —a great backdrop for a date. (Open Tu-Th 5p-9p; F-Sa 5p-10p.) 🍸 ♥

FEDERAL GRILL

10 ★★★★
$$$$ Trad'l American
MIN *536 Hamilton St.*
610-776-7600
www.federalgrill.com

This casual chic establishment is anything but an all-American eatery. The Grill is an oasis downtown—zebra-print bar stools, window-pane mirrors and understated twinkle lights give off a soothing, eclectic ambiance. The menu changes daily, featuring a refreshing twist on familiar cuisine: award-winning steaks, seafood and pastas. Downstairs you'll find a full smoking bar, complete with over three-dozen brands of cigars to choose from. If balancing a cigar with a martini glass isn't your skill, head upstairs to the dining room—great for a night on the (Allen)town. When it's available, order the deep yellow, richly flavored carrot soup, or the pepper crusted hay tuna, delectable if sushi-grade fish does it for you. The lunch menu is lighter on your wallet, and includes burgers, salads, and a light alternative to French fries called "tobacco onions." (Open M-Th 11:30a-3p, 5p-10p; F 11:30a-3p, 5p-1a; Sa 5p-1a.) ♥ 🍸 🏃

GATE 7 DINER

10 ★★★
$ Diner
MIN *845 Linden St.*
610-361-6942

When the late-night munchies strike, only a true diner will do—and the Gate 7 Diner, downtown, is the real deal. From its shiny silver siding to the classics on its menu to its 24/7 hours, the Gate 7 will satisfy the most discriminating diner connoisseur. Seriously: what is better than 3am Guns 'n Roses from your own, boothside jukebox? (Always open.)

The Fderal Grill, between 5th and 6th on Hamilton Street (Rachael Danahy)

GEO SPIRITS & CUISINE

10 ★
$$$$ Trad'l American
MIN *904 W. Hamilton St., in the Crowne Plaza Hotel*
610-530-8570

The bright and lively decor may be one of the only memorable things about this restaurant. Of course, there's also the faint smell of chlorine and the patrons in bathing suits (thanks to the hotel's nearby swimming pool) that sets Geo apart. The service is on the slow side, though the food's not bad (steak excepted). At least the prices are high. (Open M-Th 11a-11p; F-Sa 11a-midnight; Su 11a-10p.) ✸

GLASBERN

18 ★★★★
$$$$ Trad'l American
MIN *2141 Pack House Rd., Fogelsville*
610-285-4723
www.glasbern.com

The Glasbern Country Inn, set on a one-hundred acre historic farm-turned-conference center and B&B, is a welcome change of scenery. Think beams, candlelight and stone-wall rustic elegance ("smart casual" attire is required)—for a price. You'll dine on pasture-raised meats, and fruits and vegetables grown on-site. (The menu changes with the seasons to include and highlight produce that's currently available.) You order a la cart Sundays through Fridays but are limited to a four course prix fixe menu ($55 per person) on Saturdays. While everything's good, we strongly recommend the Glasbern salad and the

20 DINING

Grille 3501: fine dining on Broadway (Sara Rosoff)

oven-roasted Glasbern chicken. (Open daily 5:30p-8:30p; reservations required.) 🍸 ♥

GRANNY MCCARTHY'S TEA ROOM

20 ★★
$ Cafe
MIN *534 Main St., Bethlehem*
610-861-7631
donegal.com/tea_room_home.asp

This restaurant/snack spot/tea room is sure to make you lie back and think of England (or Ireland—whatever). Voted "best tea in the Valley" by *Lehigh Valley Magazine* for the past two years, Granny McCarthy's offers a homey ambiance with tasty treats. A variety of soups, salads, pastries, shepherd's pies, quiches, and hot and cold beverages are offered daily, and Guinness-battered fish and chips are available every Friday evening. Pass the crumpets! (Open M 11a-3p; Tu-W 11a-4p; Th 10a-8p; F 10a-9p; Sa 9a-5p; Su 9a-3:30p.) 🍶

GRILLE 3501

5 ★★★
MIN $$$$ Asian Fusion
3501 Broadway
610-706-0100
www.grille3501.com

For a little high-end dining without the trek to New York City, try Grille 3501. The food's exceptional—from appetizers like the crab and mango spring rolls ($10) and creamy crab soup ($7), to entrees like the braised beef short ribs ($22) and the char grilled filet (cooked to perfection) ($27). Legal drinkers can wash it all down with something from the extensive martini bar (how about a Staten Island "Mar-Tony"?) or classic cosmopolitan. It's a good thing the edible options are so delicious, though, because the service isn't—particularly for younger customers.

(Open Tu-F 11:30a-10p; Sa 4p-10p.)
♥ 🍸

GYROS QUEEN

3 ★★
$$ Middle Eastern
MIN *1601 Liberty St., near 17th St.*
610-433-9600

Who doesn't like a good gyro now and then? (We don't know how to pronounce "gyro" either.) This family-owned restaurant, hidden in a CVS-anchored strip mall, is a real gem. Don't be fooled by the bland decor and fake flowers: the Greek/Middle Eastern dishes are great—especially the kabobs. (We were less than impressed, though, with the Greek salad and wish there was more than just baklava for dessert.) For a big fat Greek good time, check out the private party belly dancer. (Open M-Sa 11a-9p; Su noon-8p.) 🍱

HAIKA'S KITCHEN

3 ★★★★
$ Bakery
526 N. St. Cloud St.
610-351-0005
www.haikas.com

Appropriately named, Haika's Kitchen is an intimate bakery with a distinct, homey feel. Behind the small, but powder-flecked, treat-filled display counter, the ovens and work tables are visible, as is the small friendly staff making cakes and other pastries. Hanging from above, dozens of metal utensils are suspended. Watch the decadent sweets prepared on long counters, covered in white dusty flour and rose-colored organic eggs. Haika's is proudly organic, and freshness is the rule here: the pastries' fruit fillings are bought directly from local orchards. Haika's stocks lunch and dinner options too, though everything is take-out. Especially original are their

vegetable soups, including the uniquely titled African Peanut Soup. A rich blend of vegetables (carrots, squash) mixed with a thick, velvety peanut taste, the soup coats your mouth with every sip. The soul of Haika's, though, are its Danishes, scones, cupcakes, cookies, and custom-made cakes. The bakery's health-conscious treats make it a good supplement to the Farmers Market (see page 8); and if you're looking for a mid-afternoon snack, it's within a 10 minute walking distance of the college. As their window sign says, "Life is short—eat cake." (Open W-F 8a-6:30p; Sa 8a-4p.) 🍱

HAMILTON FAMILY RESTAURANT

3 ★★
$ Diner
MIN *2027 Hamilton St.*
610-433-6452

"HamFam" is a party—at two in the morning when the only test you have to worry about is a breathalyzer. Although newly renovated, HamFam closely resembles a 1980's Michael Jackson music video. Skip the slimy browning fruit, be warned that the cheese fries are a bit oily (make that soaked in oil) and know that your large orange juice—though delicious—will be the size of the shot glass you used earlier. Focus instead on their breakfasts for a solid midnight snack. It's an experience, but don't be surprised if your designated driver insists on staying behind the wheel. (Always open!)

DINING

THE HANOVERVILLE ROADHOUSE

22 ★★★
$$$$ Trad'l American
MIN 5001 Hanoverville Rd.,
Bethlehem
610-837-1122
www.hanroadhouse.com

If you're expecting a casual and noisy Texas Roadhouse, you're in for a surprise. Housed in an historic building from the 1820s, the Hanoverville Roadhouse has a warm and homey feel: you'll be tempted to look for a doorbell as you walk across the porch and reach the old wooden door. The Roadhouse proudly displays the past with exposed beams and portraits of Abraham Lincoln and Benjamin Franklin. It's gourmet but not exotic—the dishes are traditional American fare and include prime rib, shrimp scampi, and chicken marsala. The place is a bit pricey (although well worth it) and attracts a classier, more mature crowd than the typical college joint. (Open M-Sa 11:30a-3:30p; 4p-9p; Su 3p-8p.) ♥ ⍾

HAVA JAVA

4 ★★★★
$ Cafe
MIN 526 N. 19th St.
610-432-3045

Tucked away in an old row house on 19th Street, this funky coffee shop is the soul of the emerging 19th Street "bohemia." Industrial beams hold hundreds of hanging mugs; the checkerboard, tiled floor makes you think you're in a country cottage kitchen one second and an elegant ballroom the next. If you're hungry for brunch or a light lunch, they've got homemade pies, muffins, bagels and scones to quell your appetite. Most important, though, are the brews. They know their coffee, and serve up an array of blends as well as fancier lattes and cappuccinos. Time your visit so you're not arriving with the crowd emerging from the neighboring Civic Theatre. You can bring a book, but the soothing classical music and dim lighting may be more conducive to catnapping than to getting that reading done. The menu proclaims that coffee's "far better...than wine"—how true! (Open M-Th 8:30a-11p; F-Sa 8:30a-midnight; Su 10a-10p.) ⍾ ⍾

HENRY'S SALT OF THE SEA

4 ★★
$$ Seafood
MIN 1926 W. Allen St.
610-434-2628

Though billed as "Fine Dining," a trip to Henry's is similar to voyaging to a tavern on the lower deck of a boat. Complete with ship lanterns, portraits of captains and cork wreaths, Henry's nautical atmosphere not-so-subtly hints at their specialty: seafood. The menu features scallops, shrimp, flounder, crab and lobster. Land-lovers are not forgotten, and can pick between steak and chicken dishes. (If nothing strikes your fancy, they'll fix up a special request if they have all the ingredients.) All entrees come with a trip to the salad bar, a potato dish and vegetables. While it sounds like a tremendous amount of food, moderately sized portions allow you to save room for their creamy peanut butter pie. So if your in the mood for the taste of the ocean, take a short trip over to Henry's, where you'll be sure to find what your looking for. (Open M-Th 4:30p-9p; F-Sa 4:30p-10p.) ⍾

HUNAN SPRINGS

7 ★★★
$$ Chinese
MIN *4939 Hamilton Blvd.*
610-366-8338

Widow Brown (the building's last tenant) wouldn't know what hit her. While the decor hasn't changed much (it's still a mix of homey and ski lodge), the food certainly has, and all for the better. Hunan Springs serves up dishes a step or two (or three) above your typical Chinese restaurant. Whether you're taking out or eating in, you'll have your pick between an impressive array of seafood, pork, beef, duck and lamb options, not to mention several chef specials. Try the Bo Bo Platter appetizer for two ($13)—a delicious assortment of egg rolls, BBQ ribs, shrimp toast, chicken wings, teriyaki beef and cheese puffs, served around a towering flame. This is not your father's Chinese. (Open M-Th 11:30a-10p; F-Sa noon-11p; Su noon-9:30p.) ♀ ♥ 🗑

INN OF THE FALCON

25 ★★★
$$$$ Continental
MIN *1740 Seidersville Rd.*
610-868-6505
www.innofthefalcon.com

Here's a place to treat yourself to some fine dining. This out-of-the-way location, complete with a small dining room and a bar, has an intimate feel thanks to its old-world decor and fireplace. While the atmosphere is relaxed, the dress is formal (so be prepared to look the part). The Inn offers classic dishes with an original twist, like baked Brie in a caramel glaze and flank steak garnished with balsamic ice cream. The meals are expensive but the portions large, presentation impressive, and food excellent. The service is good but very

slow, so if you're going to the Inn for dinner, plan to make an evening of it. (Open W-Sa 5p-9:30p.) ♥ 🍾

JACK CREEK STEAKHOUSE

13 ★★★
$$$ Steakhouse
MIN *1900 Catasauqua Rd.*
610-264-8888
www.jackcreeksteakhouse.com

It might not be obvious from the name, but this "steakhouse" is more of an el restaurante mexicano. You almost feel as if you're at one of those touristy restaurants in the heart of Cancun—in a good way. This family-friendly eatery along the strip in the Valley Plaza is very spacious (though you'd never know it from the outside). There's a perfectly sized bar towards the front and plenty of tables and booths (some large enough to fit 10 people) in the back. Their extensive menu—from Mexican dishes like fajitas, burritos, and tacos, to a variety of steak and seafood dishes—is bound to have something for everyone. If you're in a seafood mood, we'd recommend the grilled shrimp or the crab cakes (since they're famous for their crabmeat). So here's the bottom line: it's no five star restaurant where you'd wine and dine in style, but it's perfect for those nights when you're in more of a TGI Friday's state of mind but can't bear the thought of Friday's. (Open M-Th 11:30a-10p; F-Sa 11:30a-10:30p; Su 11:30a-9p.) ♀

JARABACOA CITY

9 ★★
$ Dominican
MIN *44 N. 8th St., at Linden St.*
610-435-0781

This small and modest but very tasty restaurant right off of Hamilton Street offers a variety of Dominican dishes. The menu is limited and similar to

DINING

other Dominican restaurants' but the portions are hardy. The roasted chicken with rice is your best bet and we'd recommend the pig's feet or hen stews for the more adventurous eaters. While the restaurant is geared toward takeout customers, there is a dining area (complete with a telenovella blaring in the background). The wait staff is friendly but service overall is only adequate. (Open daily 11a-11p.)

JOHNNY MAÑANAS

8 ★★★
$$ Mexican
MIN *PPL Plaza, 8th St. & Hamilton St.*
610-434-6100
www.johnnymananas.com

The new Tex-Mex restaurant Johnny Mañana's adds a welcome splash of color to the reviving downtown, The place is easy to miss, set back in the glass-and-steel PPL Plaza, but once you're inside, you'll find yourself thinking you're not in Allentown anymore. With its sky-high ceilings, deep mustard-yellow walls, rich, floor-to-ceiling red curtains and brightly outfitted tables, Mañana's is, well, the anti-Allentown. And the food is tasty, in a Tex-Mex sort of way. Try the la fiesta fajitas ($18)—an "especial de casa mañana"—and the guacamole appetizer ($7), perfectly seasoned. J The restaurant boasts two bars, one with a temple to flat-screen television, and daily drink specials like $3 margaritas on Mondays, $3 mojitos on Tuesdays, and $3 cosmos on Wednesdays.

JUMBARS

20 ★★★★
$ Cafe
MIN *1342 Chelsea Ave, Bethlehem*
610-866-1660

When they say "Welcome to Jumbars," they're not kidding. The inviting atmosphere—think buttercup yellow walls adorned with watercolor paintings—and the fact that every patron seems to know one another offset any discomfort from the cramped quarters. The breakfast menu includes the standards—French toast and pancakes—along with homemade bread. The whole-wheat waffles topped with strawberries and bananas ($7) are amazing. If you go for an omelet instead, be sure to add caramelized onions ($5). For lunch, both the grilled ahi tuna salad ($9) and pulled pork panini ($6.50) come highly recommended by the regulars. And don't fight dessert—it'd be a hopeless battle considering the counter is laden down with everything from sticky buns to chocolate cake. Trust us, pretty soon Jumbars will be a place where everybody knows your name, too. (Open W-F 8a-3p; Sa-Su 8a-2p.)

KING GEORGE INN

5 ★★★
$$$$ Trad'l American
MIN *3141 Hamilton Blvd.*
610-435-1723
www.kinggeorgeinn.com

Though its neighbors are Dorney Park, a mini-golf course, and several chain restaurants, the King George Inn manages to seem distant from it all. Its traditional wooden chairs, uncovered ceiling beams and lacy white tablecloths transport diners to 1756, the year the historic landmark opened. Everything is Ye Olde English at the Inn, down to the stone building itself. Keep your upper lip stiff as you

DINING

try the no-nonsense seafood and steaks, and watch your wallet: The steep prices don't mean big portions . You'll never go thirsty, though, as the wine list is exceptional. The small dining room gets packed by 7pm on a Saturday night, so reservations are a good idea. Be sure to throw on a nice shirt and pair of shoes, too—diners didn't wear hoodies at the Inn in 1756 and they shouldn't wear them now! So sit back, relax, and enjoy your expensive English meal, ol' chap! (Open M-Th 11:30a-10p; F-Sa 11:30a-11:30p; Su 3p-9p.) ♥ 🍸

KOW THAI TAKE OUT

6 ★★

$ Thai
1201 W. Linden St.
MIN 610-770-9100
www.kowthai.com

Though billed as "Gourmet Thai Food Delivery," Kow Thai's takeout leaves something to be desired—the gourmet Thai food. The limited menu offers entrees "flavored" with curry, Thai dressing or sauce, but the dishes are mostly bland—even the $7 chicken pad Thai. Besides, a takeout that requires someone to "buzz" you in does not help make the wait comfortable. The chicken satay ($3.25) is the only must: Not too spicy but flavored with a zippy peanut sauce, this chicken-on-a-stick is the closest that Kow Thai comes to gourmet. (Open Tu-Sa 11a-9p.) 🍢 🥡

The 250-year-old King George Inn, at Hamilton Bypass and Cedar Crest Blvd. (Megan Blessing)

LA MEXICANA GRILL

8 ★★★★
$$ Mexican

MIN *407 N. 7th St.*
610-776-1910

Nobody does "full" like La Mexicana Grill. This festive restaurant—with mango orange walls and year-round Christmas lights—serves up a ton...and it's all great. The fajitas (veggie, chicken, beef or shrimp) bring words like "mountainous" to mind; entrees like the chicken mole ($13) are similarly huge and tasty. And did we mention that all dinners come with two sides—like fried plantains, refried beans or sweet potatoes? We'd say save room for the main course, but that would mean missing out on the city's best salsa (an on-the-house treat, along with chips) and homemade guacamole. So just be prepared to roll your way out—it's the kind of place that the "after dinner walk" was made for. (Open daily 11a-9p.) ▮

LA PLACITA

7 ★★★★
$ Mexican

MIN *158 N. 12th St.*
610-821-4549

Who would have guessed that the best Mexican restaurant in Allentown is a cramped grocer? It's true, and we're not kidding about "cramped": La Placita squeezes in just three snug tables at the end of a narrow passage lined with hanging produce. (A sign, for the 8th Hole ("Par 4"), taunts the claustrophobic.) Prepare for sensory overload: Mexican music bounces off the flag-green walls, while tamales, sausages and baskets of avocado all compete for scarce counter space. The food makes it all OK. Trust us. The enchiladas verdes de pollo ($6.75) are divino, and we've never tasted

anything quite like the cecina con nopales (cactus with Mexican dried beef, $7.50). The $2 tacos—try the spicy pork—are blessedly affordable. La Placita put the hole in the wall, and we're damn grateful. (Open M-Sa 9a-5p.) ▮ 🗑

LAS PALMAS

10 ★★
$ Cuban

MIN *959 W. Turner St.*
610-437-1680

It's a 1950s diner, Cuban style. At Las Palmas, the portions are big (and cheap!) and the service is friendly. Try the Cuban sandwich with pork, ham, and cheese ($4), or the carnes de res frita (fried flank steak) ($8), or the tostones (fried sweet plantains) ($4). They also have delicious milkshakes—made with real fruit—and traditional chicken soup if you want to stick to something a little less exotic. Get ready to test your conversational Spanish skills and don't forget to bring cash (since they don't accept plastic). (Open daily 7:30a-9:30p.) 🗑 🧍 🛇

LATIN FLAVA

10 ★★
$ Puerto Rican

MIN *502 Gordon St.*
610-351-9793

Latin Flava has replaced the troubled nightspot Shorty's, and now the polished wood bar is one of the best places in town to enjoy pastellilos and alcapurria (both $1). Cheerful yellow and red paint, streamers and flags serve as shout-outs to this corner restaurant's Puerto Rican heritage. The menu varies daily—the friendly owner-chef is justly proud of his rotating Puerto Rican specialties, including boiled banana (75 cents) and "canoes" (long, open-faced sweet bananas packed with beef, $1.50). All of the lunch and dinner platters, including beef stew, are a steal at $5.50, and come with rice and beans. (Even the pig's feet and chicken gizzards are $5.50!) Definitely try the potato ball, a little gem of fried mashed potatoes and ground beef. The colorful, dimmed dining nook is a great place to set up with coffee or hot chocolate and your Intro to Democracy reading. (Open M-Sa 10a-7p.) 🍴

LEE'S GOURMET BISTRO

10 ★★★
$ Cafe
MIN *33. N. 9th St.*
610-432-3354
www.leesgourmetbistro.com

If you're downtown for lunch, drop by chef Lee Reinhard's eponymous bistro, just off Hamilton Street in the shadow of the PPL Building. The place is cheerful—bright yellow walls and checkered floors—but the main event is the fresh and delicious fare. Try the bagels, muffins, and pastries, but save room for the "city-style" sandwiches (double the meat) or the succulent Angus burger ($6.25). The local-produce salad bar is full of brightly-colored freshness, and the coffee, Seattle's Best, is joined by a full espresso bar. For breakfast, try "Lee's Famous bull's eye eggs" ($2) or the syrup-drenched French toast with powdered sugar ($2.50). (Open M-F 6:45a-4p.) 🍴 🍴

LITTLE SAIGON

8 ★★
$ Vietnamese
MIN *1033 N. 6th St.*
610-821-5350

Turn your head for a second and you're bound to drive right by Little Saigon, so pay attention. And you're not at the wrong place, so don't lose faith once you enter. (The Formica tabletops and sea shell wallpaper are hardly typical Asian restaurant decor.) But the friendly service and outstanding Vietnamese and Chinese fare are as authentic as they come. The Vietnamese egg roll (a non-fried version of its Chinese cousin) is an excellent appetizer choice. With the rest of the menu full of large-portioned entrees for about $6, Little Saigon is bound to appeal to both your stomach and your budget. (Open W-M 11a-8:30p.) 🍴 🍴

🐾 LO BAIDO'S

10 ★★★★
$$$ Italian
MIN *442 N. 8th St.*
610-820-7570
www.lobaidos.com

If you're heading downtown, make sure to pay a visit to this family-owned local favorite. Though the romantic music and table candles clash with the pizzeria-style open kitchen, Lo Baido's redeems itself with its friendly service and delectable Italian cuisine. Although it's BYO, expect to get a complimentary glass of their homemade wine. The food is freshly prepared with homemade sauces and salad dressings. Most entrees are served with a house salad—a mishmash of basic lettuce, ziti and raisins—and an intermezzo of homemade sorbet. The baked manicotti ($13) and the chicken marsala ($16) are especially good, as is the penne ala vodka con gamberi ($19). You won't have room, but loosen your belt and try some of the inexpensive-yet-fabulous ice cream, made fresh on site. Lo Baido's makes you feel like you're in Little Italy, thanks to its fresh, homemade ingredients and superb staff. (Open M 11a-8p; Tu-Th 11a-9p; F 11a-10p; Sa noon-10p.) 🍴 ♥ 🍴

LOUIE'S

11 ★★★
$$$ Italian
MIN *2071 31st St. SW*
610-791-1226
www.louiesrestaurant.com

Imagine the scene from the Disney classic *Lady and the Tramp*—two hound dogs sharing a strand of spaghetti with soft Italian music in the background—and you've got a perfect picture of the atmosphere at Louie's. Established by the Belletieri family in 1958, under the moniker of Gino's, Louie's is the quintessential Italian family restaurant. Recently moved to Allentown's South Side from its longtime 12th and Chew location, Louie's has had a face-lift. Black and white family photos still stare down at long tables covered with checkered tablecloths. The main attraction, by far, is the cuisine: The Belletieri's traditional home-style sauces set Louie's apart from all of its old country imitators. The sauces are so good that they sell them under the Belletieri product line. The desserts are frightfully tasty. The Italian rum cake, chocolate moose and chocolate peanut butter pie, in particular, should be illegal. (Open M-F 11a-10p; Sa 4p-10p; Su 4p-9p.) 🍴 ♥ 🍸 🎵

MAGNOLIA'S VINEYARD

17 ★★★
$$$$ Trad'l American
MIN *2204 Village Rd., Orefield*
610-395-1233
www.magnoliasvineyard.com

This secluded restaurant, in an old 19th-century country inn, certainly lets you escape the chaos of campus. The decor is surprisingly modern, though, and the food cosmopolitan. For an added twist, legend has it that a young woman (waiting for her lover to return from war) haunts the building. That may explain the short wait time between your appetizer and main course—maybe the host wants to get you moving before you encounter any wandering spirits. (Open Tu-Sa 5p-9p; Su 3p-9p.) ♥

MAMBO

3 ★★★
$ Mexican
MIN *1902 W. Allen St.*
610-351-4070

If you're in the mood for some Mexican/Spanish/Caribbean cuisine and don't feel like going far, it's Mambo to the rescue. Located just a few minutes from school at 19th and Allen Streets, Mambo offers great service and never-ending dining options—owner Johansen Hernandez is happy to tailor meals to your liking even if they're not on the menu. Start with a sample of the seasoned homemade chicken, steak, or pork. And we'd suggest the black bean with chicken soup as an appetizer and the enchilada, burrito, and tostado combination for your main course—it's a delicious and huge amount of food, all for under $10. Mambo is BYO but, if you should forget, there's a liquor store right next door. (Open M 11a-8p; Tu-Sa 10a-11p; Su 11a-8p.) 🍾 🍴

MANGOS

6 ★★★
$$$ Mediterranean
MIN *3750 Hamilton Blvd.*
610-432-4420
www.mangos-restaurant.com

The Mangos experience is hard to define—one-part Caribbean casual and two-parts Mediterranean chic. The building is unassuming and unfortunately placed, wedged between a McDonald's and a gas station, but once inside you might forget that you're in Allentown at all. Stucco walls, brick floors, dim-lit lamps, romantic table candles, columns with archways, wood paneling, and deep reds, blues, and yellows evoke Barcelona. (Don't neglect the intimate courtyard in warm weather.) Mangos is best-known, as it should be, for its tapas (appetizers that, combined, can serve as a meal) and rum bar. Try the Mojito, the restaurant's most popular cocktail—it's exceptional. The food is inventive (though occasionally a bit too salty); the paella is particularly good. The waitstaff is friendly, if a bit inefficient. Good thing it's worth the wait. (Open M-F 11a-10p; Sa 4p-10p.) ♥ ⵙ ⵣ

MARIO'S PIZZA CAFE

5 MIN
★★★
$ Italian
3335 Hamilton Blvd.
610-435-4484

Hidden in a plaza with chain giants like Subway, Friendly's and Carrabba's, this small Italian eatery is quite a find. The crackling brick-oven fire and warm orange walls create a welcoming feeling, and small tables and smiling waitstaff add to the cozy atmosphere. The menu ranges from strombolis to large stuffed pizzas to Mario's specialty, hot panini sandwiches. Best bargains at Mario's are the pasta dishes, served with a salad and basket of garlic bread, each costing 10 bucks or less. We also suggest trying the strombolis, but be forewarned-the medium can feed a small army. Whether you're taking out or eating in, Mario's is a great alternative to another evening meal at GQ. (Open M-Th 10a-10p; F-Sa 10a-11p; Su 11a-9:30p.) ⵙ ⵣ ⵤ

MELT

19 MIN
★★★
$$$$ Italian
Promenade Shops at Saucon Valley, Center Valley
610-798-9000
www.meltgrill.com

Think Melt when your taste buds are longing for a trendy twist on traditional Italian cuisine. Dining on one of Melt's three floors, you'll have your pick of creatively prepared salads, pizzas, pasta and grilled entrees. Be prepared, though, to spend some cash (entrees are pricey) and possibly leave hungry (portions are small). But hey, where else can you find a restaurant with stunning decor reminiscent of coastal Europe just a few doors down from Old Navy and LL Bean? (Open M-Th 11a-11p; F-Sa 11a-midnight; Su 11a-10p.) ⵙ ♥ ⵣ

MORGAN'S

11 MIN
★★★★
$$$ Trad'l American
3079 Willow St.
610-769-4100
www.morgansrest.net

Think country dining with a sophisticated flare. Morgan's flagstone walls and fireplaces give it the feel of a cozy cottage—not surprising since the building used to be an inn and, before that, a B&B. Good luck choosing among their delicious homemade breads, dishes and desserts. We'd suggest starting with their French onion soup or bruschetta with lump crap herb salad and lemon sauce ($10). Entrees range from filet mignon and rosemary marinated lamb chops, to parmesan crusted halibut and pan-seared tuna. Our favorite was the molasses and garlic-marinated pork tenderloin with ginger applesauce. And our top pasta pick is the papparadelle Bolognese pasta ($10 for a lunch portion and $14 for an entrée). Even their sandwiches and salads are big enough to leave you satisfied. Early birds are rewarded well here: If you can make it to Morgan's by 11am, you'll get to enjoy several different kinds of frittatas ($5), fluffy omelets ($5), and the German Apple Pancakes ($5). (Open M-Sa 7a-9p.) ♥ ☥

NAWAB

19 ★★★
$$ Indian

MIN *13 E. 4th St., Bethlehem*
610-691-0631
www.nawabrestaurant.com

Don't let the small restaurant fool you —this place has huge flavor. The walls are pepto pink (a foreshadowing of the medicine you may need later), while tacky chandeliers and fake plants hang from above. Thank goodness that their authentic Indian cuisine more than makes up for the lousy interior decorating. Nawab is a three-time winner (in 2000, 2001 and 2002) of *Lehigh Valley Magazine'* s "Best in the Valley—Indian Restaurant Award." (Okay, it's not a Nobel Prize, but it's gotta count for something, right?) Start with samosas, then try lamb rogam josh for a spicy challenge (order plenty of naan—bread—to relieve your taste buds), or the chicken tikka masala for something milder. Vegetarians, don't despair: There are plenty of meat-free meals, tasty enough even for carnivores. Be sure to bring your ID (students get 15% off lunches and dinners). (Open M-Th 11:30a-3p, 5p-10p; F 11:30a-3p, 5p-11p; Su 11:30a-9:30p.) ▐

NICK'S DINER

3 ★★
$ Diner

MIN *1802 Tilghman St.*
610-439-5070

Your mother should have taught you to never judge a book by its cover. Keep that lesson in mind during your next trip to Nick's Diner, which is small, dingy and crowded. The crowded part is easy—the place is popular and for good reason. Nick's has great food, an exceedingly friendly waitstaff and efficient service. The small and dingy part, well, that just adds to the character of this '50s-style metal-box diner, where the walls are adorned with paintings by local artists. Definitely don't miss Nick's all-day breakfast specialties, wraps and French fries, and save room for dessert. (There are over ten freshly baked pies and cakes to choose from.) Thanks to inexpensive prices and overflowing portions, you'll leave with a full stomach *and* a full wallet. (Open daily 6a-10p.)

O'BRIEN'S REALLY GOOD FOOD

3 ★★
$ Deli

MIN *1922 Allen St.*
610-435-3911

O'Brien's Really Good Food may have overshot a little with its audacious name—we're thinking O'Brien's Not Bad Food may have been a bit more appropriate. The decor of this deli reminds us of a hospital cafeteria, with muted pink, green, and beige walls and random tchotchkes arranged on each table. The elderly staff are very sweet but slow-moving. The deli selection at O'Brien's is ordinary, and the size of the kitchen leaves you disappointed that they don't offer more choices— though several homemade soups are featured each day on a rotating basis.

Overall, O'Brien's is a decent mom-and-pop kind of deli if you need a break from GQ (and who doesn't?); just don't expect that you'll be getting anything extraordinary. (Open M-F 7a-2p.) 🍴 🏃

PANERA BREAD

3 ★★
$ Cafe
MIN *3100 W. Tilghman St.*
610-432-3221
www.panerabread.com

Panera is European café meets cozy ski lodge. There's a fireplace in the main dining area, toasty on a cool autumn evening. The bakery is old world too, with a vast assortment of pastries, breads and bagels lining the wooden shelves. The sandwiches, soups and salads are inexpensive, and sometimes inventive: Try the soup in a sourdough bread bowl ($5) or the popular grilled panini sandwiches (around $7). Just don't forget to order a café mocha and a caramel pecan brownie for dessert. We promise Dr. Atkins won't come after you. (Open M-Sa 6:30a-9p; Su 7a-7:30p.) 🍴

PAOLA'S

12 ★★
$$ Colombian
MIN *102 W. Susquehanna St.*
610-791-6556

Plain on the outside, Paola's—a family-run Colombian restaurant—is downright manic on the inside, with bright yellow walls and a few tables with a view of the kitchen. Go for traditional Colombian treats like grilled tongue or beefsteak "a caballo" or stick with a simple bacon cheeseburger. The service is not that fast, but the televisions inside will keep you occupied until the huge (and cheap!) entree is served. (Open daily 7a-10p.) 🍴

PAPRIKA'S

20 ★★
$$ Hungarian
MIN *1180 Main St., Hellertown*
610-838-6570

Hellertown may be a bit of a drive, but this quaint, modest eatery makes the trip well worth it. Self-described as the only authentic Hungarian food in the Lehigh Valley, Paprika's serves up delicious, home-cooked meals. Start with the pierogis—a mixture of scrumptious fried dough, potatoes, and sour cream for just $3. There's also the Chicken Paprika's ($7), chunks of chicken and Hungarian noodles in a pool of cream sauce that's so good you'll be soaking it up with bread. Stop whining, and get in the car. (Open W-Th noon-8p; F-Sa noon-9p; Su noon-7p.)

PARMA PIZZA

3 ★★
$ Italian
MIN *3100 W. Tilghman St.*
610-439-6940

There's a reason Parma Pizza is called Parma *Pizza* and not something a little more extravagant or inclusive. It's true that the restaurant's atmosphere leaves much to be desired. And while the menu has a decent number of options—ranging from traditional Italian favorites like pasta, calzones, strombolis, subs and steaks, as well as salads—few (if any) are as good as the pizza. The pizza, though, gets high marks. There's a wide variety of toppings and specialty pizzas including taco or eggplant parmesan. Its wallet-friendly prices, close proximity to Muhlenberg (within walking distance for the car-less), and quick delivery make it convenient for students. In addition, the management is often happy to cooperate with on-campus organizations and programs. While not the choice for sit-down Italian fare, Parma Pizza is a reliable place to turn during any pizza craving. (Open Su-Th 9a-9:30p; F-Sa 9a-10p.) 🥡 🍴

PASTA ALLA ROSA

10 ★★
$$ Italian
MIN   *602 W. Hamilton St.*
610-774-9500

If you're venturing downtown to Hamilton Boulevard, consider Pasta alla Rosa for an Italian lunch. The menu consists of typical lunch items, like wraps and salads, but also various chicken, fish, or shrimp entrees. Dishes are served with pasta (with a choice of five sauces) or vegetables. Despite the crowds of lunchtime downtown employees, the place maintains a minimalist elegance, with framed Italian museum posters and checkered curtains. It's not necessary to make an exclusive trip here, but if you're in the area and craving Italian, it's worth the stop. (Open M-F 9a-4p.) 🥡

PHILLY'S STEAKS

8 ★
$ Fast Food
MIN   *1137 Hamilton St.*
610-782-0373

If you're willing to travel for a quality cheesesteak, you may want to go a bit further than this shady joint. The seating is uncomfortable at best, featuring cushions (if you can call them that) with a tacky floral print. The atrociously dim lighting gives you the "this place used to be a pub" feel (which, in fact, it was). Even if the ambiance doesn't throw you, Philly's probably isn't your best bet for high-cholesterol fare. Take the "Philly Sampler," advertised as an appetizer of two pierogis, four onion rings, four chicken nuggets, two mozzarella

sticks, five breaded mushrooms and French fries. Actually, ours came with zero pierogis, six onion rings, four chicken nuggets, two mozzarella sticks, three breaded mushrooms and French fries. But who's counting? Our final answer: Don't go out of your way for this place; they definitely won't go out of their way for you. (Open M-Th 11a-10p; F-Sa 11a-11p; Su 11a-10p.) 🥡

PISTACHIO BAR & GRILLE

3 ★★
$$ Continental
MIN   *341 S. Cedar Crest Blvd.*
610-435-7007
www.pistachiobarandgrille.com

If you've been scouring the Lehigh Valley for a trendy restaurant where you and your friends can sip martinis and look hip, you may be in luck. But with pricey, mediocre fare and inefficient service, eating at Pistachio regularly would be...well, nuts. The decor is warehouse chic, complete with exposed pipes and art deco light fixtures. Echoing acoustics turn conversations into shouting matches. The menu is hefty but don't be fooled —the salads (which occupy almost a full page) are all over $10 and a letdown. You're better off with a pasta dish or the eggplant shelbourne, which is yummy AND huge. Even if you don't have room for dessert, at least check out the tray. Worst-case scenario: You settle for a cup of Mexican hot chocolate. So if you're feeling more SoHo than Allentown, head to Pistachio with a full wallet, earplugs and patience. (Open Su-Th 11:30a-midnight; F-Sa 11:30a-2a.) 🍸

RINCON SALVADORENO

9 ★★
$ Salvadoran
MIN *958 Hamilton St.*
610-351-5153

Rincon Salvadoreno is certainly cause for celebration: The unassuming Salvadoran restaurant is kind on the stomach *and* the wallet. The empanadas are delicious ($1-$1.50), and the fried sweet plantain platter ($5.50) is the best we've tasted. The light blue walls, the long Formica counter, the plastic folding chairs, the cheerful regulars—they come together, somehow. There's a warmth to Rincon Salvadoreno—it's Cheers with a Salvadoran accent. (Open daily 10a-10p.) 🍙

RINGER'S ROOST

See NIGHTLIFE

RITA'S

3 ★★
$ Ice Cream
MIN *1918 W. Tilghman St.*
610-435-4501
www.ritasice.com

Something cold and refreshing hit Pennsylvania in the summer of 1984: Italian ice! That year, the Tumulo family made PA a little sweeter when it founded Rita's Italian Ice, which soon spread to cities up and down the East Coast, including Allentown. They claimed then to use the perfect recipe, and even today few could argue. In spring and summer, the overheated can't wait to get their hands on a "wooter" ice (that's "water" ice in Philadelphian), yogurt, custard or "misto." You'll pick from dozens of flavors, like passion fruit, peach and wild black cherry. A small will only set you back $1.15 with tax—and just one dollar more for a large. That may seem like a lot for ice and syrup, but it's worth every penny. More outdoor stand than ice cream parlor, Rita's shuts down for the winter. But when it's open, Rita's provides a uniquely chilling experience. (Open seasonal.)

RITZ BARBECUE

3 ★★
$ Barbecue
MIN *302 N. 17th St., in the Fairgrounds complex*
610-432-0952

Forget the Ritz-Carlton. The Ritz Barbecue is old-school Allentown, frozen in the 1950s. (You half expect tailfins and roller-skating servers.) The neon-clad building is right in the middle of the Fairgrounds, just to the east of the Farmers Market complex. Park your car and walk up to the service-windows, or take a seat in the diner-like interior. We ordered a meal of pork barbecue, baked beans and fries ($10), and it was worth every ounce of guilt. The place is known for its homemade ice cream, as it should be. At the Ritz, cuisine is a city in France, but that's OK. The nostalgia is free. (Open daily 11a-10p.) 🍙

ROBATA OF TOKYO

9 ★★★
$$$$ Japanese
MIN *39 S. 9th St.*
610-821-6900
www.robataoftokyo.com

Here's a laid-back locale featuring authentic Japanese cuisine—along with a bit of flare. Robata of Tokyo specializes in a Japanese style of grilling known as hibachi. And the chefs cook up more than just food, entertaining diners with their technique as they prepare entrees right before their eyes. (While it's possible to spend a solid amount of money here, the chicken hibachi includes a heaping portion of chicken, fried rice and veggies, as well as soup and a salad, for just $13.) If you're in the mood for something else, check out Robata's extensive selection of appetizers, entrees and sushi. Also, don't forget to browse the drink menu. The banzi bomber—24 ounces of fruit-and-booze deliciousness—is a house favorite despite its $10 price tag. (Open Tu-Su 5p; closing times vary.)

ROCK AROUND THE CLOCK CAFE

6 MIN ★★
$ Cafe
1301 W. Hamilton St.
610-770-1588

Who says you can't go back? This cafe makes time travel possible and worth the trip. The golden oldies on the radio and walls plastered with records and signed photographs make you nostalgic for the days when rock and roll was, well, rockin'. And if the ambiance doesn't, the menu certainly will, with options like the "Mama Cass" hot ham sandwich, the "Sittin' on the Dock of the Bay" crab patty and "You Ain't Nothin' But a Hot Dog" (Elvis sighting, anyone?). Unfortunately, this cafe certainly does *not* rock around the clock—it's closed by 2pm. But, if you're up early (they open at 7am) or looking for a new lunch spot, it's a fun and tasty place to try. (Open daily 7a-2p.)

SALVATORE RUFFINO'S BRICK OVEN PIZZA

3 MIN ★★
$$ Italian
1840 Allen St.
610-437-3621

Ruffino's isn't shy about what it does best. The specialty here is brick oven pizza, and a whole lot of it. The restaurant serves Napolitano (thin crust), Sicilian (deep dish) and stuffed (where the ingredients are between two layers of dough). And it's all cooked in an actual brick oven visible from the dining room. (Just drag your eyes away from the desserts on display and you'll see it.) If pizza's not your thing, there's also a lengthy menu full of pasta, chicken and veal entrees, as well as calzones and other sandwiches. Plus, you can't help but enjoy the atmosphere—very "Italian village" with service like you'd find in the classiest places. It's a great date spot, especially on weekends when they've got live entertainment. (Open M-Th 10a-10p; F-Sa: 11a-11p; Su noon-10p.)

SLIPPERY PETE'S EATERY

4 MIN ★★
$ Deli
345 S. Cedar Crest Blvd.
610-439-7900

For a quick and great-tasting meal, head to Slippery Pete's. The atmosphere is cozy and patrons can watch the food being prepared while enjoying Pete's amazing complimentary pickles at this quintessential deli. Breakfast is served all day and delivery is free. Best of all, Pete's has a catering menu—something to keep in mind for those not-so-distant graduation parties. Vegetarian? Don't fret. While the menu doesn't offer tons of options, Pete's veggie wrap is fantastic. (Open M-Tu 7:30a-3p; W-F 7:30a-4:30p.)

SPICE INDIA

13 MIN ★★★
$$ Indian
2407 Mickley Ave., Whitehall
610-432-0980

Finally—some Indian food right in our backyard! If you're looking for perfectly spiced Indian cuisine that won't break the bank, travel over to the new Spice India, which is nestled on a side-street off of MacArthur Avenue in Whitehall. With its spare decor and simple set-up, Spice India lets the food speak for itself. Each meal begins with flat crispy Indian crackers (and two tantalizing dipping sauces), as well as a pitcher of ice water—an oasis between spicy courses. But don't worry! Each order can be prepared mild, medium, or hot, depending on your chutzpah. The entrees are on the small side, so make sure to order at least one dish per person, or a few to share around the table. Our personal favorites: shrimp tandoori (an appetizer), chicken tikka masala, and the goat kahari (cooked with tomatoes, peppers and onions). And don't forget to order a side of Indian specialty bread, naan, baked in the tandoori oven. (Open M-F 11:30a-3p, 5p-10p; Sa noon-3p, 5p-10p; Su 8a-noon, 5p-10p.)

Salvatore Ruffino's Brick Oven Pizza, off 19th Street (Melanie Heazel)

SPOONERS

9 ★★★★
$ Cafe
MIN 921 Hamilton St., near 9th St.
484-212-9727

Spooners, in the heart of downtown, serves up delicious homemade soups as well fresh salads, sandwiches and baked treats. Opened in 2006, Spooners has a funky feel, with old posters, whicker seat chairs, and sleek hardwood floors. The daily soup and sandwich specials, made fresh by friendly owner Linda, are listed on a giant chalk board near the register. We recommend the Jail House Chili—it's meaty and delicious (but definitely has a kick, so keep the water close by). Pair it with a half sandwich, like the roast beef and red pepper or turkey and avocado, and you've got a delicious combo. And if you want to turn lunch into a full afternoon out, take advantage of the checkerboards and

checkers at every table. They've even got breakfast fare for those of you up early enough. Recently, A Cup and Such Gourmet Coffee moved in, with coffee, espresso and everything in between. Enjoy Chauncey's Roast on one of the deep sofas. (Open M-F 7a-4p.)

STARFISH BRASSERIE

17 ★★★
$$$$ Seafood
MIN 51 W. Broad St., Bethlehem
610-332-8888
www.starfishbrassiere.com

Don't worry, the tasty food at the Starfish Brassiere more than makes up for its less-than-tasty decor (bright neon sign, starfish window decals, fish statues...you see what we mean). On Sundays, the chef prepares a three course meal for $27.50. On other days of the week, order from the eclectic menu a la carte. Not surprisingly, the restaurant offers plenty of seafood options to choose from (tuna, salmon,

DINING

sea bass, even Australian Barramundi) —all priced around $23. (Open M-Th 11:30a-2:30p, 5p-9:30p; F 11:30a-2:30p, 5p-10p; Sa 5p-10p; Su 5p-8p.) �Y

THE STONED CRAB

12 ★★
$$$$ Seafood
MIN 1905 Brookside Rd., Macungie
610-398-8060
www.stonedcrab.net

The Stoned Crab is the perfect place for any seafood lover—with a little extra money to burn or parents in town. Although pricy, the Stoned Crab has a great menu of appetizers, salads, and entrees (almost all include seafood), not to mention a full service bar. If you're not in the mood for clams or oysters, try the filet mignon or their delicious Portobello fries as an appetizer. (Open Su-Tu 11:30a-9p; W 11:30a-10p; Th 11:30-11p; F 11:30-1a; Sa 4p-1a.) �Y ♥

STOOGES
See NIGHTLIFE

SUNLIGHT RESTAURANT

9 ★★
$ Latin American
MIN 801 Hamilton St.
610-770-0713

Hidden away beneath the busy streets of downtown Allentown is the Sunlight Restaurant, serving up traditional Caribbean cuisine. The inexpensive prices (breakfasts under $4, sandwiches for $3 and dinners mostly between $6 and $12) may lead you to believe that the helpings are small, but don't be fooled. The plates are piled high and every entree comes with at least one side. Make sure you try the yellow rice and finish up with flan for dessert. Just brush up on your Spanish

before you go—so you can respond to the *buenos dias* you'll be greeted with when you arrive. (Opening hours vary; call for details.) 🍟

SUNSET GRILLE

15 ★★★★
$$ Mexican
MIN 6751 Ruppsville Rd.
610-395-9622
www.sunset-grille.com

For those who want to skip the mall's chain restaurants, the Sunset Grille provides great food, attentive service, and affordable prices. Housed in an old inn, this restaurant and its friendly wait staff make you feel like a guest in a Texas home. While you won't see obnoxious cactuses or sombreros, the Sunset Grille keeps the theme with brick-red, rich blue, and teal-patterned curtains and tablecloths. Muted TV's in the corners of the dining room make the atmosphere more casual without creating a lot of distraction. The "Southwest" options (fajitas, quesadillas, and the like) are traditional favorites, but you certainly don't need to have a taste for Mexican food to fall in love with this menu—the char-grilled steaks, homemade crab cakes, and tender ribs are just a few of the great alternatives. Sunset Grille may have tried to branch out a bit too far, however, with items such as the Chinese chicken salad, so avoid these oddballs and you won't be disappointed. The bar area, while small, allows you to sit with friends and enjoy the best of both worlds-great drinks and delicious food. (Open M-Sa 11a-2a; kitchen closes at midnight.) ☓Y

DINING

SWEET ITALIAN PIZZA

10 ★★★
$ Italian
MIN   535 N. 7th St.
610-740-3833

It may be hard to spot this tiny pizza place among the other little shops on 7th Street, but what a find it is. There's nothing much to look at inside, except for a few Italy-inspired paintings on the wall, but the staff is friendly and over-accommodating. Their menu offers any Italian, and even non-Italian dish, you can imagine (including Latin specialties)—all for less than $10. Their thin pizza slices are generous, not loaded with grease (!), and very tasty. While their baked ziti and subs are what you'd expect from any ol' Italian place, the price and portion are commendable. If students are reluctant to venture out of the bubble and head downtown, free delivery is surely the way to go from this very sweet secret spot in Allentown. (Open daily 10a-10p.) 🗑 𐤊

SYB'S WEST END DELI

1 ★★★★
$ Deli
MIN   2151 W. Liberty St.
610-434-3882

If you manage to make it out of bed before 3pm on Saturday, drag yourself out the door and down the street (to 22nd and Liberty) to Syb's West End Deli. This down-to-earth deli—think flowery vinyl table cloths, friendly staff, freshly brewed coffee and country music—is the ideal place to reflect on the paper you've been putting off (and continue to avoid). Syb's offers classic comfort food as well as a few breakfasts with a twist—like the superb challah French toast. Lunches range from turkey sandwiches to Reubens to tabouleh and matzo ball soup. With a location that's literally right around the corner, Syb's is a great break from the Garden Room—one with a little more local flavor. (Open Tu-Th 8a-5p; F 8a-4p; Sa 8a-3p; Su 8a-1p.) 🗑 𐤊

TALLY HO TAVERN
See NIGHTLIFE

TEPPAN HIBACHI STEAK HOUSE & SUSHI BAR

5 ★★
$$$ Japanese
MIN   3227 Hamilton Blvd., in Dorneyville Shopping Center
610-841-4799
www.teppanhibachi.com

We're not sure what they were going for with the interior decorating at Teppan Hibachi Steak House and Sushi Bar—the bright red walls with multicolored squares scream mod but the tables adorned with bamboo plans and a wall mural with ancient geisha tea-servers, not so much. Regardless, the wait staff is friendly and fast, and the menu has an infinite number of reasonably priced sushi combinations (accompanied by pictures just in case the Japanese names trip you up). Try the maki combi, which includes three different types of sushi (all delicious), Miso soup, Ginger salad, and ice cream, all for just under $15. Teppan's is the perfect, filling, lightweight alternative to the General's Quarters. (Open M-Th 11:30a-3p, 4p-10p; F-Sa 11:30a-3p, 4p-11p; Su 2:30p-10p.) 🍸 𐤊 🗑

Wally's, home of the Texas Tommy (Rachel Frint)

TORTILLA FLAT

17 ★★
$$ Mexican
MIN *500 Main St.*
610-868-8903
www.tortillaflatinc.com

Located in the heart of Bethlehem, Tortilla Flat offers a wide range of Mexican favorites. We'd vote for the fajitas ($13). The combo meals are a great deal but sometimes it's hard to know what you're eating or taste any difference between the dishes. The changos ($4)—fried bananas with a caramel filling—are a must for dessert. The service is fast and helpful. And the hand-painted murals and the doggy cantina make both two- and four-legged patrons feel welcome. (Open M-F 11a-10p; Sa 9a-10p; Su 9a-8p.) ¥ ⚲

TSANG'S BISTRO

8 ★★★★
$$$ Chinese
MIN *2730 Walbert Ave.*
610-433-8188

Tsang's is too good for the Lehigh Valley. What we mean is that we don't deserve Chinese this good—we're not worthy! The decor is clean and tasteful, almost calming. We tried an old standby, moo shu pork, and one of Tsang's specialties, mango chicken. Both were painfully delicious. With apologies to the Buddha at the entrance, we have to add a fifth Noble Truth: This is the best Chinese in the Valley. (Open M-Th 11a-9:30p; F-Sa 11a-10:30p; Su noon-9:30p.) 🥡 ¥

TU CASA

11 ★★
MIN $$ Dominican
223 Hamilton St.
610-433-2012

¿Habla español? No? Well, then, this might not be the place for you. This is not your ordinary taco and quesadilla hotspot; it's a Dominican restaurant with Spanish-speaking regulars. Tu Casa, as the name suggests, is a casual joint, with televisions (and even a giant projection screen) blaring Spanish-language music videos and soap operas. The Spanish-only menu is potentially crippling for the monolinguists among us, but pictures of each dish make point-and-smile ordering possible. Whole fish, shrimp, octopus, steak and chicken (all mostly fried) are the menu staples, with side choices including rice and fried plantains. If you like Chi Chi's, then stick to the strip malls. We're more at home at Tu Casa. (Open M-F 11a-11p; Sa 11a-10p; Su 11a-9p.) 🍴

TURKISH RESTAURANT

11 ★★★★
MIN $ Turkish
34 N. 2nd St.
610-439- 8782

This family-run establishment—half Turkish market, half Mediterranean restaurant—is definitely one of Allentown's buried treasures. Certainly not noted for decor—a few paintings, a hanging carpet and a TV showing the latest in Turkish entertainment—the place is charming thanks to the friendly chatter of regulars and staff. And then there's the food: so good it's worth the wait that's typical at this popular spot (so don't show up starving), and *very* reasonably priced. (Entrees are all under $16 and sandwiches range from $1.35 for a burger to $4 for a lamb pita.) Whet your appetite with a hummus platter, and be sure to try the kebabs (prepared with a secret and truly "special blend" of spices). (Open daily 11a-11p.) 🍴 🗑

WALLY'S DELI

5 ★★★
MIN $ Deli
11 N. 17th St.
610-435-7177
www.wallysdeli.com

Do you like sandwiches but haven't found a deli that makes the *perfect* one? Well, nobody's perfect, but Wally's sure comes close with its hogalicious sandwiches, great salads and famous "Wally's Chips"—their own take on waffle fries. You can mix and match ingredients to concoct your own sandwich or order one of the Specialty Hogs (try a "Texas Tommy," a "Squealer" or a "Surfin' Turkey"). Be careful: The deli is snuggled next to a seafood store and behind a Citgo, so it's easy to miss. Don't be turned off by its cramped quarters—its food portions are big enough to fill even the most demanding stomach. And besides —size doesn't matter anyway... (Open M-W 9a-6p; Th-F 9a-7p; Sa 9a-6p.) 🗑

WERT'S CAFE

3 ★★★
MIN $ Burgers
515 N. 18th St.
610-439-0957

From the outside, Wert's Cafe looks like a stucco-covered block plopped down in the middle of a parking lot. This less-than-promising exterior only makes the charm hidden inside more of a welcome surprise. Walk through the doors and you enter a country ski lodge, with wood-covered walls and small tables and booths. It's almost always crowded, but don't let that deter you, since you'll be seated in no time. And the hordes are all there for good reasons. In addition to typical pub fare, Wert's also serves up plenty of appetizers, including unique creations like sweet potato fries, pretzerella sticks (pretzel-covered mozzarella sticks) and an ungodly mound of stringy onion "rings." The waitstaff is friendly and doesn't mind special requests or split bills. (Open daily 11a-10p.) 🎁

WHITE ORCHID
16 ★★★
$$$ Thai

MIN *Promenade Shops at Saucon Valley, Center Valley*
610-841-7499
www.whiteorchidthaicuisine.com

The soothing lullaby of clattering forks, light conversation, and piano music piped in over the stereo system washes over your senses at the White Orchid. The tranquil taupe walls of the wood-paneled restaurant are bathed in the flickering candlelight from each table, reflecting off the deep brown pools of sauce saturating your meal. White Orchid, in the Promenade Shops, mixes a more intimate, cosmopolitan environment with traditional Thai dishes. The menu is vegetarian-friendly, with the option to substitute vegan, and they allow you, with mercy, to set your meal's spiciness. The staple pad Thai, a noodle dish with a rich peanut taste, is given new life here, with its fresh, Caribbean after-taste. The portions, though modest, are filling, so be sure to leave room for the exotic dessert menu. Traditional deserts like crème brulee and cheesecake, at the White Orchid, are served with surprising new flavors. We recommend reservations on the weekend, as word has spread quickly about the Orchid. (Open M-Sa 11a-9p; Su 11a-8p.) 🎁 ♥ 🍸

WILDFLOWER CAFE
17 ★★★
$ Cafe

MIN *316. S. New St., Bethlehem*
610-758-8303
www.myspace.com/wildflowercafe

Perhaps no other word besides "eclectic" can do the Wildflower Cafe justice. There's a giant bamboo bar with a "happy days" sign, vintage sofas and chairs strewn throughout the small room, and artwork covering every last inch of the walls. With a menu including everything from PB & fluff to vegetarian chili to ambrosia to home-made cookies, the Wildflower feels more like your parents' basement than a music lounge and coffeehouse. While the food is nothing you couldn't make in your own kitchen, Wildflower is a great venue for live music. And if you're a musician yourself, make sure to stop by for their open mike nights on Monday and Tuesday. (Opening hours vary; call for details.) 🎵 🍶

YOCCO'S
4 ★★★★
$ Hot Dog

MIN *2128 W. Hamilton St.*
625 W. Liberty St.
610-821-8488

Like a bad elementary school joke, Yocco's, the Lehigh Valley's "Hot Dog King," is serious about its wieners. And these aren't your ordinary wieners. Since 1922, Yocco's has been dishing up dogs—cooked Texas-style, served on a bed of chopped onions, and lathered in heavy-duty mustard and a liberal application of "secret" chili sauce—to adoring fans. The now-chain began as a single shop at 625 Liberty Street, and was founded by the uncle of former Chrysler CEO Lee Iacocca. ("Yocco" is locals' mispronounced version of the family's last name.)

Beyond its famous tubes of pork and beef—actually shipped worldwide—Yocco's also serves the standard fare of hamburgers, cheeseburgers and cheesesteaks, seven days a week. A truly decadent culinary experience... just don't forget to pack a roll of Tums for the car ride home. (Open M-Th 10a-10p; F-Sa 10a-11p; Su 11a-10p.) 🍟

shell out another 15 cents for cheese!) A sprawling cheesesteak for $3.85? A full plate of buffalo wings for $3.60? When you crave no-nonsense grease for almost nothing, head to this family-owned South Allentown legend. You can't miss the orange stucco. (Open Tu-Sa 10a-10p; Su noon-9p.) 🍟

YOUELL'S OYSTER HOUSE

5 ★★
MIN $$$ Seafood
2249 Walnut St.
610-439-1203

Awkwardly named, yes. Hard to find—it's true. But we came for the seafood, and here we were impressed. The "famous" clam chowder deserves its acclaim—it's some of the best we've tasted. The Maryland crab dishes, straight from the Chesapeake, are delectable. The place is named for its oysters, and they're also tasty (and especially slippery). Our servers were friendly and astoundingly knowledgeable about the menu. (Ask about the chowder, and you'll get a rapid-fire ingredient recitation.) Youell's has a nautical elegance to its dining room, and it should: The prices here, though fair, will stretch the college budget. Parents weekend? (Open M-Th 4p-9p; F-Sa 4p-10p.)

ZANDY'S STEAK SHOP

9 ★★
MIN $ Burgers
813 St. John St.
610-434-7874

Zandy's doesn't have a website. Zandy's street-strangled orange stucco structure is flat-out ugly. Inside, Zandy's resembles a neglected, fifties banquet hall. The truth is, we wouldn't have it any other way; we like our Zandy's old school. Where else can you get a burger for $2.35? (Be prepared to

CHAIN GANG

Applebee's
1500 N. Cedar Crest Blvd.
610-530-2450

Arby's
Cedar Crest Blvd. & Tilghman St.
610-433-7220

Baskin Robbins
345 S. Cedar Crest Blvd.
610-439-7900

Bob Evans
2805 Lehigh St.
610-798-9395

Boston Market
385 S. Cedar Crest Blvd.
610-770-3324

Burger King
3105 Hamilton Blvd.
610-432-2614

China King
1901 Hamilton Blvd.
610-820-5831

Domino's Pizza
4229 Tilghman St.
610-395-1515

Dunkin' Donuts
1427 Tilghman St.
610-433-0773

Friendly's
460 S. Cedar Crest Blvd.
610-770-9883

Manhattan Bagel
3100 Tilghman St.
610-433-8555

McDonald's
721 N. Cedar Crest Blvd.
1414 Tilghman St.

Outback Steakhouse
3100 Tilghman St.
610-437-7117

Papa John's
706 N. 13th St.
610-434-7272

Perkin's
Cedar Crest & Hamilton Blvd.
610-820-5767

Pizza Hut
1448-52 Chew St.
610-776-7900

Quiznos
118 W. Hamilton
610-740-9200

Subway
1537 N. Cedar Crest Blvd.
610-434-0505
1313 Tilghman St.
610-434-5609

Taco Bell
3380 Lehigh St.
610-966-5144
2113 MacArthur Rd., Whitehall
610-437-0465

TCBY
3100 Tilghman St.
610-820-5922

TGI Friday's
395 S. Cedar Crest Blvd.
610-776-8188

DINING INDEX

DINING

DINING INDEX

DINING INDEX

Gate 7 Diner
Nick's Diner
Zandy's Steak Shop

dominican

Awilda's
El Castillo Del Caribe
Jarabacoa City
Mambo
Tu Casa

german

Dunderbak's

hungarian

Paprika's

ices/ice cream

Rita's Italian Ices
Lo Baido's

indian

Nawab
Spice India

italian

Bacio
Bellissimo
Bravo!
Buca di Beppo
Cafe Buon Gusto
Carrabba's Italian Grill
Lo Baido's
Louie's
Mario's Pizza Cafe
Melt
Parma Pizza
Pasta alla Rosa
Salvatore Ruffino's Brick Oven Pizza
Sweet Italian Pizza

jamaican

Caribbean Delight

japanese

Allentown Farmers Market
A1 Japanese Steakhouse
Robata of Tokyo
Teppan Hibachi Steak House

latin american

Amigo Mio
Awilda's
Caribbean Delight
El Castillo Del Caribe
Jarabacoa City
La Mexicana Grill
La Placita
Las Palmas
Latin Flava
Mambo
Paola's
Rincon Salvadoreno
Sunlight Restaurant
Tu Casa

live music

Allentown Brew Works
Godfrey Daniels (see page 52)
Louie's
Wildflower Cafe

mexican

Allentown Farmers Market
Amigo Mio
Cali Burrito
Cactus Blue
Jack Creek Steakhouse
Johnny Mañanas
La Mexicana Grill
La Placita
Tortilla Flat
Sunset Grille

DINING

DINING

DINING INDEX

mediterranean

Mangos

middle eastern

Aladdin
Allentown Farmers Market
Damascas
Gyros Queen
Turkish Restaurant

muhlenberg picks

Allentown Brew Works
Allentown Farmers Market
Bay Leaf
Bellissimo
Damascus
Federal Grill
La Mexicana Grill
Lo Baido's
Morgan's
Spooners
Sunset Grille
Syb's West End Deli
Tsang's Bistro
Turkish Restaurant
Yocco's

outdoor seating

Allentown Brew Works
Bellissimo
Black Orchid
Bravo!
Federal Grill
Hava Java
Las Palmas
Jarabacoa City
Johnny Mañanas
Las Palmas
Mangos
Melt
O'Brien's Really Good Food
Rock Around the Clock Cafe
Syb's West End Deli
Tortilla Flat

pa dutch

Allentown Farmers Market
Dunderbak's
Wert's Cafe

puerto rican

Latin Flava

pizza

Allentown Farmers Market
Louie's
Mario's Pizza Café
Parma Pizza
Salvatore Ruffino's Brick Oven Pizza
Sweet Italian Pizza

salvadoran

Rincon Salvadoreno

seafood

El Castillo Del Caribe
Henry's Salt of the Sea
Starfish Brasserie
Stoned Crab
Youell's Oyster House

southern

Allentown Farmers Market
Black Orchid
Caribbean Delight

soup

Allentown Farmers Market
Spooners

steakhouse

Buckeye Tavern
Charlie Brown's
Federal Grill
Jack Creek Steakhouse

DINING INDEX

NIGHTLIFE

The great thing about Allentown? It's big enough to have a range of late-night activities but small enough so that all of them are just a short walk or drive away. If you're in the mood to sit down and watch the game, pay a visit to Rookie's. If you want to dance the night away, head on down to Maingate. And, if you want a little bit of everything, the Sterling Hotel is a great choice, with karaoke, pool and live music. Whatever you choose, a good time in Allentown is always right around the corner.

ALLENTOWN BREW WORKS

See DINING

BETHLEHEM BREW WORKS

18 ★★★
$$ Brewpub
MIN *569 Main St., Bethlehem*
610-882-1300
www.thebrewworks.com

We used to trek to Bethlehem to this trendy brewpub and beer lounge, but the Fegley family opened a second location in A-town (see page 7). Still, the Bethlehem site has its own vibe. The industrial-chic upstairs bar and the dimly lit Steelgaarden downstairs (complete with votive candles, jazzy music and curvy couches) both incorporate a design element appropriate to the area's history: mix of cold, hard lines of steel, and soft, elegant decor. They brew many varieties of beer right on-site— including Valley Golden Ale and Steelworker's Oatmeal Stout. If you can't decide, just order the Sampler for a taste of each. They also have all the old stand-bys (from Bud Light to mixed drinks) as well as over 100 Belgian beers on the menu downstairs. And did we mention the food and pool tables?

(Open daily 4p-2a.)

THE BRIDGEWORKS

23 ★★
$$ Brewpub
MIN *4 E. Fourth St., Bethlehem*
610-868-1313
www.bridgeworksrestaurant.com

"The architects of food and the engineers of spirits" gather at this corner Irish pub in Southside Bethlehem. With green walls and a burnt amber tiled ceiling, this non-smoking bar-restaurant features an inviting menu of seafood, steak, pasta, chicken, and stir-fry dished up by some of the friendliest folks in the Lehigh Valley. Four beers on tap, a variety of bottled beers, specialty drinks, and wine will keep you occupied while you admire the caricatures of historic Bethlehemians among the small-town crowd. (Kitchen open M-Th 11:30a-10p; F 11:30a-11p; S 11:30a-midnight; Su 11:30a-10p; bar hours vary.)

CANDIDA'S

6 ★★★
$$ Gay Bar
MIN *247 N. 12th St.*
610-434-3071

It's that little gay bar down the street. But this neighborhood staple on the corner of 12th and Chew hardly sings queer—not the exposed brick walls, the calm lighting nor the lone pool table. Inexpensive drinks are served by amusingly opinionated bartenders who know the regulars by name. Candida's is loud and smoky on weekends, but the slow weekdays are low-decibel and conversation-friendly. Perks? Their fried food menu includes onion rings for just $1 and a fenced-in patio is open when it's warm. (Open daily 2p-2a.) ⬦ 🍴

CHICKEN LOUNGE

4 ★★
MIN $$ Bar
3245 Hamilton Blvd.
610-439-1707

Okay, so the exterior is a bit spare—windowless with a red neon sign and a mosaic chicken. And the interior features more chicken-themed artwork than should ever be stored, let alone displayed, in one place. Still, the Chicken Lounge is actually worth a visit. The tables and booths all circle around the center bar, giving the place a cozy feel. Flat-screen televisions take up any wall space not already spoken for by a chicken, and are great for game days. (Sunday football beer specials and giveaways help, too.) The alcohol selection is average for a bar of this size, and the menu is quite extensive and less chicken-focused than you might think. You can get anything from salads to bison burgers. Definitely try the nachos...few people

don't rave about the heaping plate of chips (actually Doritos) smothered with cheese, salsa, guacamole, sour cream and peppers. Service is fast and friendly, but feel free to linger in the lounge; customers go for the social atmosphere rather than the cozy dining experience. Don't be afraid to relax and get messy—you'll blend right in with the crowd. (Open daily 11a-2a.) ⬦

CROCODILE ROCK

7 ★★★
MIN $$ Club
520 Hamilton St.
610-434-4600
www.crocodilerockcafe.com

The website boasts that it is the "Lehigh Valley's largest rock 'n roll multiplex club," and it's probably true. A haven for concertgoers, Croc Rock attracts a mix of nationally recognized big names and local bands. The slightly seedy vibe is fun, in a local color kind of way. Croc Rock offers the standard drinks, dancing and food, but the big attraction here is the music scene. And the concert tickets are as cheap as $10. Brave patrons can even live out rock-star fantasies by showcasing their karaoke skills. The combination of cheap drinks, good music, and great friends will make a

NIGHTLIFE

LEGEND

🐏 MUHLENBERG PICK	MINUTES FROM CAMPUS, BY CAR	**8**	
$ DRINKS LESS THAN $3	DRINKS BETWEEN $6 & $10	**$$$**	
$$ DRINKS BETWEEN $3 & $5	DRINKS OVER $10	**$$$$**	
⬦ BAR FOOD	LIVE MUSIC	♫	
💰 COVER	OUTDOOR SEATING	🍸	

visit to Croc Rock one of your more memorable nights at Muhlenberg. (Open M-Sa 5p-2a.) ◈ ♫ ◉

THE FAIRGROUNDS HOTEL
3 ★★
$ Bar
MIN 448 N. 17th St.
610-433-7630

The Fairgrounds Hotel is an intriguing little hole-in-the-wall bar that comes attached to a somewhat classier restaurant. A far cry from the adjacent club Maingate, this little bar full of rich mahogany and Allentown regulars serves as a satisfying change to the usual Liberty Street Tavern or Stooges crowd. The maroon- and green-striped wallpaper does the old Victorian hotel proud, but allows the tacky neon beer lamps to stand out more than ever. Happy hour brings out cheap drinks and even cheaper appetizers, such as the Fairgrounds Sampler and the always delicious mozzarella sticks. During the warmer months, the outdoor porch is an inviting place for a cold beer as the old Victorian building properly serves as an escape—a change of scenery. Just try not to become a regular amid this older crowd who are, no doubt, far beyond their college days. ◈ ⚉

THE FARMHOUSE
See DINING

FEDERAL GRILL
See DINING

GODFREY DANIELS
19 ★★★
$$$ Folk Club
MIN 7 E. 4th St., Bethlehem
610-867-2390
www.godfreydaniels.org

We should mention right off that beverages at Godfrey Daniels are strictly non-alcoholic. That's OK, because future music legends (tomorrow's Woody Guthrie or John Lee Hooker) may be glancing at you from a shady corner of the room. Called a "non-profit member supported listening club," this place sounds more like a support group for music addicts. In fact, it resembles a folksy coffee house. The saloon-like lettering and worn wood panels in the front window are a good indication of Godfrey Daniels' warm and intimate atmosphere. Music lovers of all sorts can enjoy the entertainment here, where "folk" music means bluegrass, blues, country, jazz and even Celtic. With tickets pushing $20, a show here is not always a bargain; then again, you never know when you may be paying $12.50 to hear the next Muddy Waters. (Box office open daily 2p-6p.) ◈ ♫ ◉

JABBER JAWS
4 ★★
$ Bar
MIN 1327 W. Chew St.
610-432-6524

Dive bar chic at its finest. Jabber Jaws isn't much on the eyes, service, or selection, but it is a decent choice for Allentonians looking for a live music scene or a quick game of billiards. The patrons are friendly locals, but don't make Jabber Jaws your first choice on most nights; you can find better right around the campus. The cheap drinks are one of the only pluses, as draft beers are only $1.50 on any night.

The Chicken Lounge. Enough said (Sara Rosoff)

During the warmer months, there is limited outside seating—on church pews!—with a nice view of Chew Street row houses. So if it is live, local rock music that you crave, take a look at Jabber Jaws. Otherwise, take a look somewhere else. (Open M-Su 2p-2a.)

JACK CALLAGHAN'S

3 ★★★
MIN $$ Bar
2027 Tilghman St.
610-432-5797
www.jackcallaghans.com

With two hundred dollars and a taste for unique and exotic beers, you too can be a legend at this Allentown watering hole. Jack Callaghan's Ale House looks just like any old Irish pub, with its share of Guinness and Bass paraphernalia on the wall and Kelly green furniture, but this is a place of quiet challenge. Callaghan's is home to the infamous "Beer Mug Club," marked by the 400-plus pewter mugs hanging

J.P. O'Malley's, off 15th Street (Craig Kind)

over the bar. To join, you have to drink each and every beer the place stocks (from Flying Fish to Hoegaarden) for the right to claim your own mug. Fear not if beer isn't your thirst quencher of choice: The bartenders have a steady hand with the typical swanky drinks like cosmopolitans and margaritas. The fact that the crowd is heavy on locals and lighter on students is part of the beauty of this establishment. If you want to escape the familiar faces, Callaghan's gives you the chance to try unusual beers without the threat of running into that sketchy guy from your math class. (Open daily 4p-2a.)

J.P. O'MALLEY'S

4 ★★★★
MIN $$ Bar
1528 Union St.
610-821-5556

O'Malley's takes happy hour to the next level. With $3 domestic pitchers and $6 imported pitchers on "college pub nights" (Tuesdays and Thursdays from 5pm to midnight), think more along the lines of ecstatic. Mid-week you can also get a basket of wings for only $2. (Disclaimer: They're not joking when they say "hot" wings. Don't think you're a tough guy; take the server's advice. But if you just can't help yourself, go for the kryptonite wings... just don't say we didn't warn you.) Whether or not you're focused on quantity, there's plenty of quality here, too. If you feel like introducing your taste buds to something more sophisticated than Bud Light,

O'Malley's boasts an impressive 35 different beers on tap, 15 domestic bottles, 20 imported bottles and 28 microbrews. And did we mention that the food menu's delicious and cheap? (Open M-Sa noon-2a; Su noon-1a.)

JELLY BEANS SOUTHSIDE JAM

15 ★★
$ Bar
MIN *1996 S. 5th St.*
610-797-2477
www.jellybeansouthjam.com

If it wasn't located so far (about a 15-minute drive) from campus, Jelly Beans could easily become a regular stop on the Muhlenberg bar scene. Even with the distance, it's a contender. Jelly Beans boasts a 50-seat bar, almost ten TVs (including a made-for-the-playoffs 60-inch Hitachi Ultravision) and a room for video games, pool and darts. There's a steady stream of classic rock from a DirecTV satellite music system, as well as 80s dance music every Friday. And menu items (like sandwiches, burgers, salads and a variety of "munchies") are all under $10. There are so many reasons to venture to the "Southside" that it's well worth the extra travel time. (Open M-Sa 7a-2a; Su 11a-2a.)

LIBERTY STREET TAVERN

1 ★★★★
$ Bar
MIN *2246 Liberty St.*
610-740-3888

While the name might change, the watering hole at the corner of 23rd and Liberty is consistently a favorite stop for beer-hopping 'Berg students. Stubbornly called "Woody's" by the faithful, Liberty Street Tavern—a small pizza and beer joint—packs 'em in like sardines almost ever night. Monday night is karaoke, Tuesday is trivia, and

Wednesday brings 50 cent slices and $5 pitchers. Entertain yourself while you're guzzling down pitcher with three MegaTouch games, a pool table, a ring toss game and a juke box. Whether you're stopping by for a quick bite and a brew, or partying the night away, Liberty Street Tavern's the place where "everybody knows your name." (Open M-Th 11a-1a; F-Sa noon-2a; Su 11a-midnight.)

LUPO'S

3 ★★★
$$ Bar
MIN *2149 Reading Rd.*
610-820-5570
myspace.com/luposbeefandale

If finding a youthful and hip watering hole is your mission, Lupo's will disappoint. But if you want $4 pitchers and a night with middle-aged locals, you have found heaven. Despite its older "townie" feel, Muhlenberg has a tendency to take over Lupo's on the weekends. The bar features cheap drinks, pool tables, a digital jukebox and a good-sized deck to escape the smoke-filled interior. Lupo's also offers daily food specials, including cheesesteaks, burgers, and spaghetti. Forgive the lackluster decor and initial shadiness: Lupo's is fun with a big group of people. A word of advice: When ordering a mixed drink, be sure to specify a brand. Lupo's has a tendency to make you think you're drinking nail polish remover instead of rum or vodka. (Open daily 11a-2a.)

MAINGATE

3 ★★
$$ Club
MIN *17th St. & Liberty St.*
610-776-7711
www.maingatenightclub.com

A little club on the corner of the Allentown Fairgrounds, Maingate is not a night in the Village or a party with the crew in Philly. The tunes are monotonous and the dance floor's the size of your typical dorm room. Plus, your fake ID and Victoria's Secret lace "cami" (the one you insist is a shirt) won't guarantee you entrance—take it up with the bouncer. Still, it's fairly close to campus and, once in a blue moon, Maingate opens its doors to the 18- to 20-year-old crowd. Check Facebook for updates, and be prepared to dish out the cash to get in. (Open Th 10p-2a; F 6p-11p; Sa 9a-2a.) 🍸 💰 ♫

MEDINA'S HOTEL GRAND

10 ★★
$ Bar
MIN *46 N. 10th St.*
610-433-8883

Your first instinct on entering Medina's may be to turn around and walk straight out the door. But give this beer-serving hideaway a chance. Think of it as Allentown's version of Cheers— widely popular in the Spanish-speaking community, you quickly get the sense that people come here to go "where everybody knows your name." The crowd, diverse in age and nationality, is more than happy to welcome you to their second home. Meet the owner, who will quickly introduce you to everyone in the place, pull over chairs for you, and regularly check back to make sure you're having fun. The DJ, sitting at a laptop in the corner, asks for requests but mainly sticks to rap and Latin music. The wood-floored bar, which recently moved from another downtown location into the Hotel Grand at 10th and Linden, boasts a pool table where you can play with the resident experts if you're up to the challenge. If not, ask Mr. Medina to teach you dominos and he'll be delighted to pull out his set featuring the Puerto Rican flag and share his uncanny genius. (Open Tu-Th noon-midnight; F-Sa noon-2a; Su noon-midnight.) ◀▶

MIXX

7 ★★
$$ Bar
MIN *801 N. 15th St.*
610-437-3970

Many patrons are so focused on the pins at the Rose Bowl that they miss the attached Mixx. That's bad news for country music lovers or line dancing fans, since Mixx is right up your... well...alley. Formerly TK's Corral, the bar features live country music on Fridays, and line dancing on Mondays and Wednesdays. Scared you're going to strike out on the dance floor? No worries: Mixx offers lessons at 7:30pm. They break from country for karaoke on Tuesdays and Thursdays, and Rock/Blues Night on Saturdays. While Tuesday is "college night" (no cover charge and $1.50 drafts), Mixx usually draws an older crowd. For the average college-aged bar-hopper, it's likely that you'd only stop in to cap a night of bowling or if you're craving some good ol' country. (Open Su-Th 6p-midnight; F-Sa 6p-2a.) ♫

The swanky bar at Grille 3501 (see page 20) (Sara Rosoff)

MONTANA WEST

26 ★★
MIN $$ Club
1030 N. West End Blvd.,
Quakertown
215-529-6070
www.clubmontanawest.com

Montana West offers some high-energy nighttime entertainment—and a healthy dose of the heartland. The club hosts Country Dance Parties three times a week, and even offers classes to help folks brush up on their line dancing. They mix it up with a little classic rock (thanks to cover bands— happy to kick back with fans after the show—and guest DJs) on Thursdays and Fridays. And College Party Nights start at 9pm on Wednesdays— complete with $1 drafts. So saddle up for the trip out to Quakertown, and don't forget your cowboy hat (or a first aid kit if you're set on riding the

mechanical bull). (Open W 6p-2a; Th 7p-2a; F 9p-2a; Sa 7p-2a; Su 5p-9p.)
💰 🎵

O'MALLEY'S

See J.P. O'MALLEY'S

P.J. WHELIHAN'S PUB

7 ★★★
MIN $$ Bar
4595 Broadway
610-395-2532
www.pjwhelihanspub.com

It's no Dublin tavern, but P.J.'s is a wee bit of Ireland right down Broadway. There's no chance of feeling cramped or claustrophobic at P.J.'s—with its wrap-around, sit-down bar and three additional rooms with tables. A somewhat older crowd enjoys the pleasant atmosphere and friendly service, and its popularity can translate into a lengthy wait for seating. Still, this joint is ideal if you're in the mood for great bar food and more than a dozen domestic and international beers on tap. Whether you're here to kick back and watch a game on one of the many TVs, or to unwind with friends over a basket of their famous wings, at P.J.'s you're lucky and charmed. (Open M-Sa 11a-2a; Su noon-midnight.) ◆

RINGER'S ROOST

3 ★★
$$ Bar
MIN *1801 Liberty St.*
610-437-4941

This once fake-ID party spot has been transformed into a more mature yet unpretentious restaurant/bar. Top picks for hungrier patrons include $5 cheeseburgers and classic munchies like potato skins or a heaping plate of nachos. The eclectic decor that lines the walls makes the whole place comfortable; no interior designer has ever set foot inside the Roost. While the Roost's three cramped rooms (a dining room and bar, and a third room somewhere in the middle) provide settings for just about any mood, this local destination may not be a place for wild and crazy partying. Still, cheap drinks and quality bar food make Ringer's Roost a solid choice for a mid-week kick back. (Open M-Sa 11a-2a; Su noon-midnight.) ◆

ROOKIE'S

7 ★★★★
$$ Sports Bar
MIN *1328 Tilghman St.*
610-821-848

Rookie's—a laid-back bar with a distinctly "sporty" vibe—is a perennial favorite among both Muhlenberg students and area residents. On

football Sundays, enjoy $2 drafts and a game (shown on any one of the approximately 15 televisions). Not that the place is overwhelmingly sporty—it's just got a mock scoreboard marquee and lighting fixtures fashioned from football helmets. Still, there's room for the non-jock. They've got live entertainment, and excellent food and drink specials. On Mondays, enjoy 2 for 1 burgers, with seasoned curly fries. And don't forget to sample Rookie's famous wings. (They're on special—all-you-can-eat for $9—on Tuesdays.) (Open M-Th 11a-1a; F-Sa 11a-2a; Su 11a-11p.) ◆

STAHLEY'S CELLARETTE

17 ★★
$ Bar
MIN *1826 Hanover Ave.*
610-432-7553

If you like the charm and personable service of a local dive bar, then Stahley's is the place for you. With great drink specials and an already inexpensive drink menu, Stahley's laid-back atmosphere welcomes anyone looking for a place to just relax and have a drink or play pool. Hungry? Stahley's is always serving food, including their famous Dyna Bites (fried broccoli with cheddar cheese), burgers, wings, pizza, hoagies, and more. And, if a bar isn't your idea of a good time, then stop by Stahley's Saturday mornings from 7am to 10:30am and order off their breakfast menu. (Open M-Sa 7p-2am.) ◆ ♫

THE STERLING HOTEL

11 ★★
$$ Club
MIN *343 W. Hamilton St.*
610-433-3480
www.thesterlinghotel.com

The dark and dingy atmosphere of the Sterling Hotel may put you off at first, but the broodiness eventually grows on you. It helps, too, that the Sterling has karaoke and live music, not to mention relatively cheap food and drinks, as well as nightly specials. The bar spans two levels, one of which includes a large dance floor, and spills onto a covered deck off of the second floor. Call ahead and they'll accommodate your private party. (Open W-Sa 5p-2a.)

STONEWALL

9
★★★★
$$$ Gay Bar
MIN *28 N. 10th St.*
610-432-0706
www.clubstonewall.com

If you're seeking a sophisticated queer-eye spot, take your fairy dust elsewhere—this neighborhood gay joint remains untouched by anything resembling the Fab Five. Named for the famed New York bar—birthplace of the modern gay rights movement—Allentown's version includes a club downstairs, with all the indispensable clubbing accoutrements: a respectable dance floor, two full bars, lights and lasers, all backed by a DJ spinning the best of Mariah/Toni/Whitney/Pink dance remixes. Upstairs in the "Moose Lounge," down-to-earth bartenders mix drinks whose flavors don't always fuse. The mounted moose head, pool tables, wall TVs, a lit grand piano—it all makes for one big feng-shui faux-pas. The live music runs from Barry Manilow to show tunes, and diners can choose from an array of deep-fried fare, sandwiches and salads. While Saturdays tend to draw an older crowd, College Thursdays (18 to party, 21 to drink)—complete with a drag show—are the most popular. Don't miss Halloween here: It's the club's biggest night of the year. (Open (Moose Lounge) Tu-Su 7p-2a; (Stonewall Bar) W-Th 10p-2a; F-Sa 9p-2a.)

Rookie's, the quintessential sports bar on Tilghman Street (Melanie Heazel)

STOOGES

2 ★★★★
$$ Bar
MIN *2101 Liberty St.*
610-432-7553

It's a place where the bouncer always knows your name and the bartenders are always glad you came—especially on Wednesdays for "Yuengs and wings." A staple on the Muhlenberg party scene, Stooges attracts locals and students alike. A restaurant by day, this nighttime hot spot's also a great place to watch a game, listen to music and catch up with friends over a moderately priced pint. The front room is all bar, or almost (since the actual bar, a large rectangular pit, takes up more than half of the room). Two small steps—which become challenging after a pitcher or two—lead into the dining room where most of the college-aged patrons set up camp. The drink menu features all the standard beers as well as a few exotics thrown into the mix (Franziskaner, anyone?). If hops and barley aren't your bag, opt for a martini instead, made with a strong hand and in a stylish glass. Either way, Stooges is a great place to have that mid-week refreshment. (Open daily 11a-2a.)

TALLY HO TAVERN

22 ★★★★
$$ Bar
MIN *205 W. 4th St., Bethlehem*
610-865-2591
www.thetallyho.com

The Tally Ho Tavern is one of PA's oldest and most popular taverns. Neighbor to Lehigh University, Tally Ho is by definition a college bar and proud of it. If you want to get away from the monotony of 'Berg bars, take a trip to Bethlehem to enjoy a night at the Tavern. The bar is split into three sections: a room with pool tables and arcade games; a traditional bar with dark, carved wood tables and booths for eating; and a large dance floor with a tiki bar. On Wednesdays, join Lehigh students for some karaoke, and dance the night away to the beats of Tally Ho's own DJ on Thursday, Friday, and Saturday nights. The drinks are reasonably priced and the pub grub is the best we've tasted—try the juicy burgers on the raised deck in the summer. (Open M-Th 3:30p-2a; F-Su 11:30a-2a.)

VOLPE'S SPORTS BAR

4 ★
$$ Sports Bar
MIN *1926 Tilghman St.*
610-432-0146
www.volpessportsbar.com

Although situated just a few blocks from campus, most students use Volpe's for a liquor store rather than a nighttime hang-out. This is probably a wise choice for several reasons. Among its detractions: Volpe's attracts an older crowd, its "entertainment" is limited to its drink list, and it just can't hold a candle to nearby competitors (like Stooges), where students are actually welcomed instead of just stared at. In the end, this sports bar doesn't seem to be sporting anything other than a local buzz. (Open daily 11a-2a.)

WOODY'S

See LIBERTY STREET TAVERN

NIGHTLIFE INDEX

best bar food

Allentown Brew Works (see page 7)
Bethlehem Brew Works
Bridgeworks
Federal Grill (see page 18)
J.P. O'Malley's
Ringer's Roost
Rookie's
Stooges
Tally Ho Tavern

beer selection

Allentown Brew Works (see page 7)
Bethlehem Brew Works
Jack Callaghan's
J.P. O'Malley's
P.J. Whelihan's
Stooges

beyond allentown

Bethlehem Brew Works
Bridgework
The Farmhouse
Godfrey Daniels
Montana West
P.J. Whelihan's
Tally Ho Tavern

clubs

Crocodile Rock
Maingate
Montana West
Sterling Hotel
Stonewall

college crowd

Liberty Street Tavern
Lupo's
Maingate
J.P. O'Malley's
Rookie's
Stooges
Tally Ho Tavern

dancing

Crocodile Rock
Maingate
Mixx
Montana West
Sterling Hotel
Stonewall

gay/lesbian

Candida's
Stonewall

karaoke

Crocodile Rock
Lupo's
Maingate
Montana West
Sterling Hotel

live music

Allentown Brew Works (see page 7)
Crocodile Rock
Godfrey Daniels
Jabber Jaws
Lupo's
Montana West
Stahley's Cellarette
Sterling Hotel
Stonewall
Tally Ho Tavern

muhlenberg picks

Allentown Brew Works (see page 7)
Federal Grill (see page 18)
J.P. O'Malley's
Liberty Street Tavern
Rookie's
Stonewall
Stooges
Tally Ho Tavern

outdoor seating

Allentown Brew Works (see page 7)
Bethlehem Brew Works
Candida's
Jabber Jaws
Fairgrounds Hotel
Lupo's
Maingate
Tally Ho Tavern

sports bars

Rookie's
Volpe's

OUT & ABOUT

L ooking for something to do on a Saturday afternoon? Tired of hanging out in Seeger's? Out of procrastination ideas? You've come to the right place. Trust us when we say that there's more happening in the Lehigh Valley than you might think. Athletes, artists, movie buffs and naturalists—entertain your every whim without venturing too far off campus. Use the following listings to find out which destinations are worth your precious time—time, after all, which could otherwise be used for a nap.

EVENTS CALENDARS

IT'S HAPPENING IN ALLENTOWN

email prelovsky@allentowncity.org to receive weekly email newsletter

LEHIGH VALLEY METROMIX

lehighvalley.metromix.com/events

LEHIGH VALLEY ARTS CALENDAR

www.lvartsboxoffice.org

LEHIGH VALLEY VISITORS BUREAU CALENDAR

lehighvalleypa.org/visitors/calendar

MUHLENBERG CALENDAR

shrek.muhlenberg.edu/Calendar

MORNING CALL EVENTS

www.mcall.com/entertainment

WDIY CULTURE CALENDAR

www.wdiyfm.org/calendar

FESTIVALS

SEPTEMBER

THE GREAT ALLENTOWN FAIR

2 MIN
17th St. & Chew St.
610-433-7541
www.allentownfairpa.org

Come one, come all to the Great Allentown Fair! For seven days only, during the first week of September, the 154-year-old Allentown Fair is in full effect. Lights, games, rides and funnel cake attract people of all ages, from across Pennsylvania. You can try your luck at a carnival game, enter a Yocco's hot dog eating contest, or buy a ticket to the grandstand for big-name musical acts. If you have a kid with you (or if you're the kid), stop by the petting zoo and let a sheep eat funnel cake out of your hands. Don't miss the Barnyard Olympics. When the Fair leaves town, though, make sure you stick around. The Fairgrounds are always hopping with the famous three-day-a-week indoor Farmers Market, complete with fresh local produce, specialty foods and a startling array of sausage products (see page 8). The adjacent Agricultural Hall hosts frequent themed shows, from antiques to dog breeders. And the Fairgrounds' Grandstand hosts famed musicians (Lynyrd Skynird, ZZ Top and Kid Rock) all year round.

CHILI PEPPER FESTIVAL

36 Bowers
610-944-8417
MIN www.pepperfestival.com

Can you take the heat? Prove it at the annual Chili Pepper Food Festival—heaven for anyone with a taste for spicy food. Vendors from the greater Allentown area (like Bowers Hotel, Thai International Foods, Old Cider Mill Herbs and Vinegars, and the Fleetwood Pepper Company) display their fiery creations for taste-testing. (There's ice cream, too, to help your mouth cool off.) Believe it or not, you can even purchase pepper crafts and clothing. Those who are brave enough can participate in the pepper-eating contest, and true pepper fanatics can pick their own at nearby Meadow View Farm.

FALL FESTIVAL & CORN MAZE

19 9941 Schantz Rd., Breinigsville
610-395-5655
MIN www.grimsgreenhouse.com

Feel like getting lost? Try the four-acre corn maze, the highlight of Breinigsville Fall Festival. The elaborate maze (made of seven-foot-tall corn stalks) takes a different shape each year—from witches to flowers to barns. Directionally challenged individuals beware: It can take as long as two hours to navigate (although gifted folks make it through in about 30 minutes) and they *do* keep score (you'll get a time card when you start). If you're failing miserably, a man in a scout-post overlooking the maze will assist with a yell or two (only mildly embarrassing). If you're really brave, test your skills during flashlight maze nights, a spooky alternative to a daytime visit. Though the Fall Festival is mainly geared toward young children (think face painting, a tricycle course and wagon rides), the water balloon slingshot appeals to the older set, as do the maze and the food (fresh kettle corn, home-made jam, pumpkin cakes, and pies). If you're looking to get lost for the afternoon, this 15-minute ride is well worth the trip. (Open Sept.-Oct.; call for hours.)

OCTOBER

OLD ALLENTOWN HOUSE TOUR

9 www.allentownpa.org/lights/
history.htm
MIN

Tour a series of restored 19th-century brick rowhomes in downtown Allentown. Local resident-preservationists open their carved wooden doors just once a year, so put this one on your calendar.

OUT&ABOUT

LEGEND

 MUHLENBERG PICK   MINUTES FROM CAMPUS, BY CAR   **8**

(Melanie Zachariades)

DECEMBER

CHRISTMAS IN BETHLEHEM

17 www.bethlehempa.org/
MIN attractions/christmas.jsp

Follow the North Star to Bethlehem—or at least the "star" mock-up that sits atop South Mountain. Bethlehem is charming any time of the year, but the city puts on its tourist best to celebrate its erstwhile native son. Visit the website for an extensive listing of events—from historic walking tours to horse-drawn carriage rides to the Christkindlmarkt craft fair. There's even some religion: Bethlehem is home to the Moravian Church in America, and the Moravian Museum features the Church's Christmas traditions throughout December.

LIGHTS ON THE PARKWAY

6 www.allentownpa.org/lights/
MIN history.htm

Every night, from late November to early January, Allentown's Little Lehigh Parkway (see page 78) gets drenched in light. Christmas lights, actually. It's much more impressive than it sounds: For $5-9 (depending on the night), you and your car gain access to a slow-moving caravan that winds its way past a startling number of lit forms. Your dorm-room Christmas bush can't compete.

MAY

MAYFAIR

1 *Cedar Beach Park*
610-437-6900
MIN www.mayfairfestival.org

Ah, May... the cold of winter is a distant memory; the stifling humidity still seems far off; seniors are prepping for and celebrating through graduation; and everyone's itching for summer vacation. For Allentonians, it's time for Mayfair. This arts festival showcases the work of area sculptors and painters, features musical and theatrical performances, and even includes a few science-related exhibits. But it's not all look-but-don't-touch. Get your hands dirty working on art projects or stuffing your face with foods (from you-name-it-on-a-stick to desserts to classic carnival favorites). So check out the art, use your creativity to make some of your own, and savor the fair foods.

JUNE

KUTZTOWN GERMAN FESTIVAL

30
MIN

Kutztown
888-674-6136
www.kutztownfestival.com

Want to explore your German roots? Don't head to the airport; you'll get a crash course in all things German, served up Pennsylvania Dutch-style, at the Kutztown German Festival. The week-long event showcases Teutonic food, folklore and fun. Bring plenty of dough because you'll want to taste everything you see—from the sausage sandwiches and ox roasts, to the pies and pastries. While you're chomping away, you'll be traveling back in time for a first-hand glimpse at traditional PA Dutch living (the dialect, the farming techniques, the social gatherings). Music, comedians and dancers combine a bit of the past with the present. And over 200 craftsmen will tempt you with quilts, homemade soaps, jewelry, clothing and more. With all this tradition and culture, you'll feel like you've ended up in Germany after all.

JULY

LEHIGH VALLEY BLUES FEST

9
MIN

9 Whitehall
610-261-2888
www.lvbluesfest.com

Each July, some of the nation's hottest blues artists meet right here in the Lehigh Valley for a four-day musical celebration. Along with the major entertainers who headline each evening, locals can test their chops at the festival's popular open jam. And it's about more than the music: The

Lehigh Valley Blues Fest is a non-profit entity, so any proceeds from ticket sales (admission is $4 on Thursday to $12 on Saturday in advance, $7 to $15 at the gate) not spent on the festival get donated to charity. One past benefactor was Dream Come True, a local organization that fulfills the wishes of terminally ill children. So let your love of the blues help lessen someone else's.

SPORTS FEST

1
MIN

Cedar Beach Park
610-439-8978
www.sportsfest.org

Remember field day from elementary school? Now picture it lasting three days, including over 40 events (from staples like basketball and soccer, to more creative selections like ping pong, arm wrestling and yoga), and utilizing all of the city's recreational facilities. Tada! You've got Allentown's annual Sports Fest. Each July, thousands of Allentonians test their skills on the field, mat or court (sign up to participate on the website), or just use the festival as a great excuse to spend some time outdoors in one of the city's amazing parks. Whichever way you play it, we're all jocks at Sports Fest.

AUGUST

MUSIKFEST

17
MIN

Bethlehem
610-332-FEST
www.musikfest.org

What has 600 bands and food from around the world, lasts for ten days, and is attended by over one million people? Bethlehem's MusikFest! The annual festival showcases up-and-comers and stars alike, belting out music of all types. Don't forget the visual artists and craftspeople, who sell their work alongside exotic food booths, where you can pick up a snack for your stroll through the Blumplatz, an 81- by 23-foot floral display. Save some energy for the Polka Jam Dance-Off. And bring a jacket: MusikFest is open rain or shine.

CULTURE

MUSEUMS & HISTORIC SITES

ALLENTOWN ART MUSEUM

9 *31 N. 5th St.*
610-432-4333
MIN www.allentownmuseum.org

Just $2 buys you access to over 11,000 works at the Allentown Art Museum, the Valley's arts nerve center. The main floor holds an eclectic permanent collection spanning 700 years (from the fourteenth to the nineteenth centuries), all in one majestic room. Modern works, a wall of gems and an underused auditorium are downstairs. The temporary exhibits are the real highlight: Recent shows include "Paths to Impressionism: French and American Landscape Paintings" and "A Different Touch: Women Printmakers from Three Centuries." For the artistically challenged, museum staff provide guided tours of the exhibits every Sunday, and guest lecturers and artists host discussions on Wednesdays and Sundays. The Met this isn't, but the museum deserves a visit at least once over your four years here. (Open Tu-Sa 11a-5p; Su 12p-5p.)

LEHIGH VALLEY HERITAGE CENTER

9 *Penn St. & Walnut St.*
610-435-1074
MIN lchs.museum

Here's an indoor activity that won't cost you a dime and just might teach you something. The Lehigh Valley Heritage Center provides visitors a glimpse into local history—including the area's natural development, immigration patterns, and urbanization. Recent exhibits included a major Hess's retrospective and "Harry Clay Trexler: The Man, the Visionary Builder, and the Legacy" (a small shrine to Allentown's legendary—and zealously worshiped—philanthropist). The museum is run by the Lehigh County Historical Society and housed in the brand new Heritage Center at Penn & Walnut (right next to Trout Hall, the place where Muhlenberg was born). (Open M-Sa 10a-4p; Su 11a-4p.)

LIBERTY BELL SHRINE

9 *622 Hamilton St.*
610-435-4232
MIN

Hold on a minute. Isn't the Liberty Bell a Philadelphia thing? Brace yourselves, folks, here comes a little history lesson...The Liberty Bell did ring in Philly to celebrate the signing of the Declaration of Independence. However, things weren't so peachy for the new nation a year later, and the patriots worried that the Brits might ransack the Bell for ammunition. To protect it, they snuck it to Allentown and hid it under the floor of Zion's Reformed Church until Philadelphia was secure. That one-time hiding place is now a shrine, complete with a life-sized replica of the Bell, flags of the original thirteen colonies, and a wall mural depicting Pennsylvania during the Revolutionary War. While the nation may have forgotten Allentown's pivotal role in its founding, Allentonians certainly haven't—they even re-enacted the Bell's trek in honor of the country's 200th birthday in 1976. (Open M-Sa noon-4pm.)

OUT&ABOUT

TROUT HALL

9 *414 W. Walnut St.*
610-435-9601
MINwww.lehighcountyhistoricalsociety.
org/trout.html

This is where it all began—Allentown and Muhlenberg both. The modest stone house, at 4th and Walnut Streets, was built in 1770 as a summer estate for James Allen, son of the city's founder. The house was sold, in 1848, to the Allentown Seminary, which became Muhlenberg. The College remained here, downtown, until 1904, when the present West End campus was occupied. There's nothing dorm-like about the current Trout Hall, which has been restored and elegantly furnished. (Open June-Aug. Tu-Su 1p-4p; April-May & Sept.-Nov. Sa-Su 1p-4p.)

THEATER

BAKER CENTER FOR THE PERFORMING ARTS

0 *Muhlenberg College!*
484-664-3333
MIN www.muhlenberg.edu/cultural/
baker/baker.htm

Often times it seems as though Muhlenberg students fail to see entertainment even when the College puts it right in the middle of campus. Enter the Baker Center, better known as "The CA" in 'Berg lingo. The CA and adjacent Trexler Pavilion hold Empie and Baker Theaters, the Martin Art Gallery, classrooms, studios, and the "Fishbowl," where window-walls allow for one of the best views on campus. Both student and faculty-directed productions take place here, and when there aren't any shows to see, the high, airy ceilings and quiet atmosphere are great for studying or looking at new student-made art exhibits.

CIVIC THEATRE (19TH ST THEATRE)

3 *527 N. 19th St.*
610-432-8943
MIN www.civictheatre.com

There's just something about that Art Deco building on 19th Street that catches your eye. Maybe it's the shabby chic exterior or the carnivalesque elephant heads or the sparkling marquee... something is bound to draw you to the home (since 1957) of the Civic Theatre. Even if the facade doesn't grab you, the inside should—the walls cloaked in burnished fabric, all that gold and copper detailing and, of course, the entertainment. This 500-seat former Vaudeville theater performs overtime, offering an annual Main Stage season of five plays and musicals, the Theater for Young Audiences and the 19th Street Film Series (featuring independent art films as well as the occasional mainstream picture). The live shows may not be Broadway, but they're entertaining and reasonably priced, with student tickets starting at just $6. To round out a night "on the town" (and within walking distance of campus), wander across the street to Hava Java café (page 22) before heading home.

MUNOPCO

6 *514 N. Poplar St.*
610-437-2441
MIN www.munopcomusictheatre.com

MunOpCo Music Theatre is the essence of community theater—family-friendly Broadway musicals without the Broadway budgets. The theater, which has been in around in one form or another since 1927, puts on three or four shows a year; recent productions include *Nunsense* and *Hello, Dolly!* MunOpCo performs at the imposing

Scottish Rite Cathedral at 1533 Hamilton Street.

STATE THEATRE

32 *435 Northampton St., Easton*
MIN 800-999-STATE
www.statetheatre.org

Although it now looks like a grandiose Broadway theater, this Easton landmark has survived through decades of decline. The State Theatre is the great Lehigh Valley comeback kid. The 1920s Vaudeville hall, by the 60s and 70s, was limping along as a B-list concert venue. In the 90s, it took $4 million to restore the theater back to its original grandeur. Today, over 90 live performances appear on its gold-trimmed stage each year, yielding about 100,000 visitors. The elegant box seats on the side of the stage are especially coveted. But be warned: You may be accompanied by someone other than your date. Starting in the 70s, patrons have repeatedly sighted a ghost, since dubbed "Fred," the spirit of the late manager J. Fred Osterstock. In memory of Osterstock, the local high school music awards ceremony gives "Freddies" to victors. Hailed as the Lehigh Valley's best place for theater, the State is an exceptional piece of saved history that will make any visitor feel nostalgic.

THE THEATRE OUTLET

610-820-9270
www.theatreoutlet.org

Here's a weekend activity that may actually *increase* your brain power. For a thought-provoking, off-campus/"Off-Broadway" experience, take a look at what the Theatre Outlet has on stage. This "theater with an edge" showcases talented local professionals and amateurs (including Muhlenberg professors, students and alums) in a mix of provocative contemporary plays

The Lehigh County Courthouse, built in 1828

and neglected classics—all for about the price of a movie ticket. It's currently nomadic, but well worth tracking down.

ZOELLNER ARTS CENTER

20 *420 East Packer Ave., Bethlehem*
MIN 610-758-2787
www.lehigh.edu/zoellner

Lehigh University's Zoellner Arts Center is Bethlehem's shining star of cultural life, hosting over 100 performing and visual arts events every year. Eclectic doesn't even begin to describe the variety—past shows ran the gamut from Fiddler on the Roof, to Cyndi Lauper, to Romeo and Juliet (by the St. Petersburg Ballet Theater). And patrons get more than just an evening's entertainment—the Center offers curtain warmers, backstage tours and *prix-fixe* dining specials at neighboring restaurants, among other "extras." Though it means venturing into enemy territory (go Mules!), it's definitely worth the trip. (Open M-F

11a-6p; Sa 11a-2p & 2 hours before curtain.)

PENNSYLVANIA PLAYHOUSE

16 *390 Illicks Mill Rd., Bethlehem*
610-865-6665
MIN www.paplayhouse.org

This nonprofit theater has emerged, since its founding in the 60s, as one of the best-known local theater companies in Pennsylvania.

MUSIC

ALLENTOWN BAND

610-437-1116
www.allentownband.com

Put "Allentown" and "music" in the same sentence, and you expect "Billy" and "Joel" to follow. It turns out, however, that A-town's musical fame dates back before 1983. In fact, the Allentown Band, formed in 1828, is the oldest civic band still around in the U.S. The ensemble's 65 members range from high school students to senior citizens, and the troupe plays all over the place (including West Park; see page 79).

ALLENTOWN SYMPHONY ORCHESTRA

9 *23 N. 6th St.*
610-432-6715
MIN www.allentownsymphony.org

The Allentown Symphony Hall, built in 1896 and known as the Lyric Theatre for most of its life, is arguably the musical nerve center of the Lehigh Valley. Its elegant facade, designed in part by the famed architect J.B. McElfatrick, has long been the public face of the Allentown Symphony Orchestra, which bought the Hall in

The Allentown Band plays summer concerts in the bandshell in West Park (Philip Johnson)

1959. The Orchestra itself, now in its 56th season, packs a surprisingly diverse range of music into its short, sporadic season. The Symphony Hall also hosts a jazz cabaret series and other special events.

BACH CHOIR

19
423 Heckewelder Pl., Bethlehem
MIN 610-866-4382
www.bach.org

The world-renowned Bach Choir of Bethlehem, the oldest such choir in America, has been belting Bach since 1898. The 95 volunteers who make up the Choir perform throughout the year (and around the world), culminating in the annual Bethlehem Bach Festival in May.

MAUCH CHUNK OPERA HOUSE

33
14 W. Broadway, Jim Thorpe
570-325-0249
MIN mauchchunkoperahouse.com

This musical venue in the beautiful mountain village of Jim Thorpe dates from the late 19th century—when citizens of the wealthy town built the "Opera House" to attract top Philadelphia talent north. It later became a Vaudeville hall, with Al Jolsen and Mae West among hundreds of well-known entertainers to pass through. After years of decline—the building even housed a pocketbook factory—the Opera House was restored in the 1970s, and live music was heard here once again. Today, an eclectic mix of acts—from bona-fide opera troupes to bluegrass to ensemble comedy to folk—performs at the Hall for rock-bottom prices year-round.

ALLENTOWN FAIRGROUNDS

See PAGE 64

GODFREY DANIELS

See NIGHTLIFE

ZOELLNER ARTS CENTER

See PAGE 71

ART

ALLENTOWN ART MUSEUM

See PAGE 69

THE BANANA FACTORY

20
25 W. 3rd St., Bethlehem
610-332-1300
MIN www.bananafactory.org

Once a banana distribution warehouse, the Banana Factory is now the Lehigh Valley's largest and funkiest arts center. Its mission is to "kindle, support and celebrate the artistic, cultural, and creative spirit of the Lehigh Valley," and by all evidence it's working. With practicing singers and kids' art classes in the background, visitors can admire both nationally renowned and up-and-coming artists in the Binney & Smith and Banko Family Room Galleries, as well as startling digital photography in the adjacent Digital Imaging Center. Upstairs, artists busily create in a suite of studios, though they'll make time to talk to visitors. On "First Fridays"—the first Friday of every month (see below)—the Factory offers free public art classes and, the rest of the year, a range of art programming for a fee. (See www.bananafactory.org for an up-to-date schedule. Open M-Th 8:30a-9p; F 8:30a-7p; Sa 9a-5p; Su 11a-4p.)

BAUM SCHOOL OF ART

9 MIN

510 Linden St.
610-433-0032
www.baumschool.org

The Baum, located across from the Art Museum on 5th Street downtown, is a thriving community art school. Its David E. Rodale Gallery hosts a rotating set of exhibits of local and regional art.

FIRST FRIDAYS BETHLEHEM

19 MIN

Bethlehem
www.bethlehempa.org

Bethlehem's South Side stays up late on the first Friday of every month. From 7pm to 10pm, everything is open: the Monsoon Gallery, the Banana Factory, craft stores, Tallarico's Chocolate shop (!) and others.

MONSOON GALLERY

20 MIN

11 E. 3rd St., Bethlehem
610-866-6600
www.monsoongalleries.com

If you're longing for fine art—particularly sculpture—and not looking to head out of the Valley, consider venturing to Southside Bethlehem to experience the cultures of Monsoon Gallery. Hosting regular art shows that feature a mix of local and world-class talent, Monsoon has been featured in the *New York Times*. The owners of the Monsoon Gallery claim this place is as deeply cultural as the weather system the name "Monsoon" describes. So if you can't find the culture you're yearning for at Muhlenberg...it may be a car ride away in Bethlehem. (Open M-Th 10:30a-6p; F 10:30a-7p; Sa 11a-6p; Su noon-5p.)

ART 'N SOUL STUDIOS

10 MIN

516 W. Hamilton St.
610-433-4850
www.art-n-soulstudios.com

Art 'N Soul combines tattoo parlor with art gallery, in the heart of downtown. A strange combination, perhaps, but consider their motto: "Where fans can enjoy the artwork of some of their favorite artists AND where an enthusiast can actually become a living canvas." A recent exhibit: Punk's Dead, featuring paintings of Sid Vicious, Joey Ramone, Wendy O Williams, and others. This is not your father's Allentown, and the city's better off for it. (Open M-Th noon-9p; F-Sa noon-10p.)

MOVIES

AMC TILGHMAN SQUARE 8

9 MIN

4608 Broadway
610-391-0780
www.amctheaters.com

For the latest movies without the sticky floor, try AMC Tilghman. It's easy to get to by car or Muhlenberg shuttle (which makes frequent trips there). And, at this nine-screen theater, you can catch the latest release for less, thanks to the student discount (just show your Muhlenberg ID). The snack bar, of course, is overpriced—and there's no student discount for popcorn.

BECKY'S DRIVE-IN

20 MIN

4548 Lehigh Dr., Walnutport
610-767-2249
www.beckysdi.com

If you're here for the summer months, or have time to make the 20-minute trip late in the spring semester, Becky's might be the perfect place for a study

Allentown's Symphony Hall is in the 1896 Lyric Theatre (Sara Rosoff)

break. Voted one of the "10 Best Drive-Ins Worth a Detour" in the *New York Times*, Becky's is much more than just a drive-in. Its movies are mostly geared towards children (PG and PG-13), and Becky's has grass for patrons to picnic on during movies. Open for business since 1946, Becky's prides itself on good service, and looks as though it's anything but your typical movie theater. (Open in summer.)

BOYD THEATRE

18 1830 W. Broad St., Bethlehem
610-866-1521
MIN   www.theboyd.com

In the world of the Boyd, movies are films, theatres are palaces, and the whole affair is a spectacle. While it only has one screen and shows just a single picture (which is readily available in

numerous other theatres), the Boyd offers substance that multiplexes cannot begin to tap. Its grand ornamental lighting and Art Moderne decor set it apart from the manufactured feel of modern chains. If the enhanced experience itself isn't convincing enough, the ticket and snack bar prices are lower than the chains—and who can turn down saving a few bucks?

CARMIKE 16

14 700 Catasauqua Rd.
610-264-9694
MIN   www.carmike.com

The Carmike 16 Theater used to be very appealing because it offered twice as many movies as the much closer AMC 8. With the opening of the Rave Theater at the Promenade Shops, though, the Carmike's average seats, consistently untidy lobby, and unfortunate location (its random position tucked behind a grocery store and Friendly's on Airport Road) have definitely bumped it down to the number two spot in the Lehigh Valley. However, if the Carmike's available showtimes suit your schedule better than the Rave's, definitely hit it up— once you find the place, you'll enjoy a movie at the Carmike just as much as you would at any other average theater. And don't worry: their snack selection is up to par, which is probably the most important element of seeing a movie anyway.

CIVIC THEATRE (19TH ST THEATRE)

See PAGE 70

EMMAUS THEATRE

19 *19 S. 4th St., Emmaus*
610-965-2878
MIN   www.emmaustheatre.com

With an old-fashioned marquee out front, the theatre gives a moviegoer the feeling of stepping back in time when going to the movies was truly a night-on-the-town. Originally a nickelodeon, the Emmaus is now a cinema that shows two films a week (two on the weekend and one during the week). The films are shown after their original release, which is perfect for that hit movie you swore you were going to see but somehow still managed to miss. The theatre is small, giving you a break from those multiplexes you somehow always manage to get lost in, and the ticket price is unbeatable ($4 adult tickets for night shows and $3 for matinees).

RAVE MOTION PICTURES

16 *Promenade Shops at Saucon Valley, Center Valley*
MIN   610-709-8635

Rave is the new kid on the block—the 16-screen, stadium-style multiplex at the end of the Promenade Shops' "main street."

SHANKWEILER'SDRIVE-IN THEATRE

16 *4540 Shankweiler Rd., Orefield*
610-481-0800
MIN   www.shankweilers.com

Think drive-in movie theaters suffered extinction before you were born? Think again. Fifteen minutes from Muhlenberg in Orefield is Shankweiler's, America's oldest operating drive-in theater. The second of its kind to open in the U.S., Shankweiler's combines the quintessential drive-in experience with today's technology: Movie soundtracks are broadcast over FM and AM radio. During spring and summer months, the theater offers a double feature for a mere $6.50 a ticket—a steal on a college budget. No evening is complete without a trip to the fully stocked concession stand, with hot dogs and buttery popcorn. This one-of-a-kind, celestial cinema is a dating must. (Open weekends in April and May; daily June-August.)

SPORTS & RECREATION

BASEBALL

LEHIGH VALLEY IRONPIGS

12 MIN
Coca Cola Park
1050 IronPigs Way (off
American Parkway)
610-841-PIGS
www.ironpigsbaseball.com

The first pitch has finally been thrown! Allentown is now home to a AAA baseball team, the IronPigs. (Yes, the name is unfortunate, but at least they're the Phillies' farm team.) The gleaming ballpark on the edge of town opened in the spring of 2008, and we've been sitting out in the grass beyond center field ever since (with tickets just $6). Reserved seats are a bargain, from $7 to $14. Beer, hot dogs, and mascot antics: how much do you love minor league baseball?

BOWLING

PLAYDROME ROSE BOWL

6 MIN
801 N. 15th St.
610-437-4606
www.playdromebowl.com

Whether you think you should be in a league, or you're the one laughing at those engraved, personal bowling balls, the Playdrome Rose Bowl has something for everyone. For the bowling pros (or at least the wannabes) the Rose offers 36 lanes with automatic scoring so you can perfect your game without counting. Once the competitive edge wears off, channel your inner child at the arcade next to the snack bar, with favorites like burgers, hotdogs, grilled cheese and french fries. (Beware: they are surprisingly pricey.) Wind down at Mixx, the attached country/western bar (see page 56). Whether it's a serious challenge you're looking for, or you just need to blow off some steam with friends, the Rose Bowl is sure to be right up your alley. (Open M-W 11a-midnight; Th-Sa 9a-2a; Su 9a-midnight.)

CITY PARKS

ALLENTOWN ROSE GARDEN

1 MIN
Parkway Blvd. & N. Broad St.

It's easy to exercise in the gleaming new addition to the Life Sports Center, but sometimes you need a change of scenery. Literally. On a crisp, sunny day, there's no spot more serene than the Allentown Rose Garden, just a few minutes' walk from campus. The garden itself is meticulously tended, laid out in resplendent symmetry and dotted with vined trellises, statuary and a white gazebo. The garden overlooks a pair of lilly-padded ponds, shaded by willow trees and bound by the wandering Cedar Creek. The whole magnificent landscape rivals Central Park's manicured beauty, but here in Allentown you may well have the place to yourself.

ALLENTOWN ARTS PARK

10 MIN
5th St., off Hamilton St.

Opened in 2007, the park is beautifully landscaped, and surrounded by a mural-clad back of the Symphony Hall, the Art Museum, the old Courthouse, and the Baum School.

BUCKY BOYLE PARK

9 MIN *Front St. & Gordon St.*

Bucky Boyle is a well-kept secret, hidden behind the factory ruins and abandoned rail tracks along Front Street. Let the crowds assemble in Trexler Memorial: One of Bucky Boyle's virtues is its post-industrial serenity. The just-renovated park overlooks the Lehigh River, and hosts, strangely enough, Lehigh University's boat house. There's a kind of covered bandstand perched above Lehigh's docks that's begging for a spring barbecue.

CANAL PARK

13 MIN *E. Hickory St., off of E. Hamilton St.*

Though it's hard to find—follow the signs once you cross the Lehigh River on Hamilton Street—Canal Park is a gorgeous, untrampled band of park on the Lehigh's northeast bank. (Follow the winding access road under a rusty rail bridge and get out to wander.) In the fall, South Mountain explodes in orange and red, rising across a sun-bleached river. Wander up and down the toepath, between the river and Lehigh Canal. You can hike or bike all the way to Easton; the round-trip to Bethlehem is only 14 miles. If you hear a rumble as you head east, it's the adjacent, sprawling freight yard; even Canal Park's tranquility has its limits.

CEDAR BEACH PARK

1 MIN *Ott St. & Hamilton Ave.*

It's finals week. Stress levels are high enough to burst the infamous "Muhlenberg Bubble." Relax. A remedy is closer than you think. Check your stress at the "red doors," and head over to the nearby Cedar Beach Park. Just a block away from campus, this oasis of lakefront greenery feels a world away. Get distracted here by playing basketball or beach volleyball. Take a stroll through the nearby Rose Garden, or along the willow-lined Cedar Creek. Or if it's rest you seek, bring along a blanket for a quick, sun-drenched nap. Host a barbecue using the park's grills, or organize a game of frisbee. Don't shy away from the park in winter, either: Cedar Beach offers the closest outdoor ice skating.

LITTLE LEHIGH PARKWAY

8 MIN *Little Lehigh St., off Martin Luther King, Jr. Blvd.*

The Little Lehigh Parkway looks like a perfectly painted picture taken directly off the wall of a country cottage and brought to life. A paved pathway winds along the Little Lehigh River, across covered bridges, and through 999 acres of green space. This vast park provides plenty of room for bikers, joggers, dog-owners, fishermen and picnickers. The park is especially bright around Christmas time (see page 66). Although parking is available, it is limited and can fill up quickly on sunny days. So stake your claim early and enjoy a beautiful day at the Parkway.

TREXLER MEMORIAL PARK

5 MIN *Cedar Crest Blvd. & Parkway Blvd.*

Trexler Memorial Park—named for and donated by General Harry Trexler—is the perfect escape after a stressful week of classes and studying. Almost half of the park's 134 acres are landscaped, providing plenty of space

Why bowl alone? The Playdrome Rose Bowl (Katie Olson)

to picnic, study or enjoy a game of frisbee with friends. Exercise fanatics can choose between two walking/jogging loops that wind (for about 1.5 miles) throughout the park; they're open to bikers on Tuesdays, Thursdays and Saturdays. Nature lovers will revel in the wildlife, as the park attracts many species of waterfowl each year. With all the greenery, it's easy to overlook the Spring House, built in 1741 on what would become Trexler's estate, and recently restored to its original appearance. In a city where everything down to the dust is named after the General, Trexler Memorial reigns over Allentown's celebrated park system.

WEST PARK

4 *West St. & Turner St.*

MIN

Whether you're planning a quiet picnic with a date or some outdoor fun with friends, West Park's your spot. More of a town square, this was the city's first park and today provides a breath of fresh air in the center of the West Park Historic District. While you're there, relax with a book near the fountain or wander past hundreds of native and exotic shrubs in the park's six-and-a-half acre arboretum. When spring rolls around, check out the beautiful displays at the annual Tulip Show. And the Allentown Band (see page 72), as well as local theater and religious groups, perform in the historic band shell throughout the summer. So the next time you need a break and some

Cedar Beach Park, below campus (Janette Tucker)

scenery, head straight to West Park—it's one more reason to love the miniature metropolis you now call home.

CLIMBING

CATHEDRAL ROCK CLIMBING GYM

27 *226 S. First St., Lehighton*
610-377-8822

The Cathedral Rock Climbing Gym facility is in an old 1842 church. Rock climbing is spiritual, right? Cathedral has over 6,000 square feet of wall for climbers to scale.

CYCLING

BIKE LINE

4 *1728 Tilghman St.*
610-437-6100

BLUE MOUNTAIN SPORTS

33 *34 Susquehanna St., Jim Thorpe*
MIN 800-599-4421
www.bikejimthorpe.com

LEHIGH VALLEY VELODROME

15 *1151 Mosser Rd., Trexlertown*
610-395-7000
MIN ww.lvvelo.org

DIVING

DUTCH SPRINGS DIVING

19 *4733 Hanoverville Rd., Bethlehem*
MIN 610-759-2270
www.dutchsprings.com

No one would deny that this place is bizarre, but that's part of the fun. Scuba dive in and around old cars and a "lost ship," or take a slide into the refreshing water. Did we mention the "sky challenge"? We were curious too.

$10 admission. (Open M-F 10a-6p; Sa-Su 8a-6p; April through November.)

FISHING

LITTLE LEHIGH FLY SHOP

8
MIN

2643 Fish Hatchery Rd.
610-797-5599
www.littlelehighflyshop.com

A fully stocked fly shop in a gorgeous 19th century stone springhouse, alongside the Little Lehigh River—in whose currents swim the largest population of wild trout in Pennsylvania. The expert staff offers lessons and guide for fairly reasonable prices. (Open M-Tu 9a-5p; Th-Su 9a-5p.)

LEHIGH RIVER GUIDES

28
MIN

146 S. 8th St., Lehighton
610-379-5460
www.lehighriverguides.com

PA FISH & BOAT COMMISSION

Lehigh County Guide
www.fish.state.pa.us

GYMNASTICS

PARKETTES

9
MIN

410 Martin Luther King Blvd.
610-433-0011
www.parkettes.com

Parkettes, the nationally famous breeding ground of gymnastics talent, trains future Olympians at its sprawling facility downtown, just off 4th Street. The gym, within its block-long warehouse-like complex, boasts an impressive alumni roll, with over 100 members who made the United States National Team, six Pan-American Team

Members and nine World Championship Team Members. Jodi Yocum (1976), Hope Spivey (1988) and Kim Kelley (1992) took Parkettes all the way to the Olympics. The gym doesn't just cultivate Olympic-caliber talent: Parkettes offers a range of classes to Lehigh Valley residents of all ages.

HIKING & JOGGING

BUSHKILL FALLS

66
MIN

Bushkill
570-588-6682
www.bushkillfalls.com

Ever wanted to see Niagara Falls, but never quite made it to upstate New York? Well, the Bushkill Falls are only an hour away, in the Pocono Mountains to the north—and they're just as beautiful. Crisp, golden brown leaves crunching under your feet, cozy warmth shining from above and the rush of mountain snow water gushing below stimulate all your senses. Trails, bridges and paths lead to seven magnificent waterfalls snuggled deep in the woods. Make sure to bring a good pair of hiking boots, as well as a waterproof camera—for that misty Kodak moment.

ALLENTOWN HIKING CLUB

www.allentownhikingclub.org

APPALACHIAN TRAIL

25
MIN

Route 309, at Blue Mountain Restaurant
www.nps.gov/appa/

Don't even think about bringing your sneakers. The Appalachian Trail is not for cheaply made brands. Dig deep in your closet for those stiff, ankle-high hiking boots—you know, the ones you bought four years ago on your "I'm-going-to-be-more-nature-loving" kick.

OUT&ABOUT

Only 30 minutes north on Route 309 is a hike on the good ol' A.T. Of the 2,158-mile stretch of trails, about 230 miles etches its way through the farm-infested Pennsylvania countryside. You may want a swimsuit if you come across one of the 22 waterfalls along the seven-mile stretch in the northeastern Ricketts Glen State Park. Beginning in the Delaware Water Gap to the north, and continuing south through Cumberland County and into Maryland, the AT hits its halfway mark at the Pine Grove Furnace State Park, just outside of Harrisburg. A tradition among hikers who travel the entire trail, known as thru-hikers, is to celebrate the halfway mark by eating a half-gallon of ice cream from the local general store. The closest access point from Allentown is about 15 miles north on Route 309, next to the Blue Mountain Summit Restaurant. (For more info, check out www.fallinpa.com, and follow the hiking and biking link.)

DELAWARE WATER GAP RECREATION AREA

65 www.nps.gov/dewa

MIN

Looking for outdoor fun to take place of your typical lazy Sundays? Take a day trip to the Delaware Water Gap National Recreation Area. In just one hour you find yourself in one of the more stunning river valleys in the country. Tons of companies cater to visitors, and it's easy to arrange canoeing, kayaking, boating, fishing, and swimming. There are more than 100 miles of hiking trails, including 27 miles of the Appalachian Trail.

HAWK MOUNTAIN SANCTUARY

43 *1700 Hawk Mountain Rd., Kempton*

MIN 610-756-4468
www.hawkmountain.org

The name says it all: Hawk Mountain Sanctuary is a safe haven for the thousands of hawks that soar through the Appalachian Flyway in east-central Pennsylvania. This conservatory of American land allows visitors a year-round nature experience. It has eight miles of trails, from the South Lookout only 300 yards from the visitors center, to the River of Rocks —three challenging miles. The Sanctuary spans 2600 acres and makes up one of the largest protected forested lands in southern Pennsylvania. Don't miss the live owl demonstrations at the visitors center. (Open daily 9a-5p; $5 admissions to the trails.)

IRONTON RAIL TRAIL

15 *3219 MacArthur Rd., Whitehall*
610-437-5524

MIN www.irontonrailtrail.org

The Ironton Rail Trail was purchased from the Lehigh Valley Railroad in 1882 and used by Thomas Iron Works to transport coal, iron ore, and limestone. Remnants from this bygone era are present along the many trails, which are great for walking and ideal for biking. Races and events take place throughout the year, including a 10K race, historical hikes, and trolley tours. If you opt to explore on your own, be sure to pick up a trail map at the Whitehall Township Bureau of Recreation. The loop portion of the trail offers a six-mile trek, with several side trails and relic sights along the way. Pack a lunch and picnic by the Lehigh River or explore the many abandoned sites, including the Coplay cement mill and the historic Lehigh

County Troxell-Steckel House. Both locations house museums. The trails are mostly paved with stone, and no motorized vehicles are allowed, so be sure to wear comfortable walking shoes and some sunscreen for this historic excursion away from Allentown.

LEHIGH CANAL TRAIL

See CANAL PARK, in CITY PARKS

LEHIGH GORGE TRAIL

34 *Near Jim Thorpe*
570-443-0400
MIN www.geocities.com/womgene/
Thorpe/thorpePage.htm

Astonishingly beautiful. Breathtaking. Trust us.

ICE SKATING

LEHIGH VALLEY ICE ARENA

10 *3323 7th St., Whitehall*
610-434-6899
MIN www.lehighvalleyicearena.com

Whether you're an avid ice skater or just someone looking for a change of pace, the Lehigh Valley Ice Arena will have you gliding back for more. While home to area ice hockey, figure skating and speed skating teams, the arena graciously clears the ice of pros for the amateur—those of us who are a little less graceful on skates. Admission and skate rentals will put you back less than the price of a movie ticket—it's a great way to get more thrills and spills for less. (Opening hours vary; call for details.)

CEDAR BEACH PARK ICE SKATING

1 www.allentownpa.org/
cedarbeach_iceskating.htm

Bushkill Falls (Antarctica Nguyen)

LASER TAG

PLANET TROG

19 *3578 MacArthur Rd., Whitehall*
610-776-8764
MIN www.planettrog.com/laser.html

Do you want relive the days when you had no care in the world? Then a visit to Planet Trog may be in order. With the largest laser tag facility in the United States (they claim) and an all-natural, 18-hole miniature golf course, Planet Trog will likely keep you busy for an afternoon. For $7 you and your friends can get out your final exam aggressions on each other in the wildly confusing laser tag complex. Complete with arcade, snack bar, and 17-foot television, Planet Trog reminds us that we are all just big kids at heart. (Open M-Tu, Th 6p-9p; Sa noon-10:30p; Su noon-7:30p.)

The green at Dorney Square Miniature Golf (Katie Olson)

MINIATURE GOLF

PUTT U MINIATURE GOLF

13 *5200 Route 309, Center Valley*
610-798-9800
MIN www.puttu.com

Putt U is a well-maintained two-course miniature golf venue—though not, as its name suggests, a school for the pros. The two courses mean that there's usually no wait, and both are lengthy and challenging. Though it's set on the edge of the highway, you feel like you're in a world of your own, safe as can be—except on Halloween. During October, Putt U blares tunes like "It's Raining Men!," but the courses are dressed with glow-in-the-dark balls, skeletons, skulls and witches. (Beware the employees: They too are costumed to scare.) With a reasonable admission and themed courses, Putt U is a gem for miniature golfers of all ages.

DORNEY SQUARE MINIATURE GOLF

3 *102 Hamilton Blvd.*
610-432-8101
MIN

If you like mini golf, Dorney Square is the place to go. Their 18-hole course is set in gardens and waterfalls—no cheesy animals and windmills here. Mini golf can be a hot date and don't worry: in the summer Dorney Square has a misting system to keep everyone cool. September brings glow golf and on Fridays, Saturdays and Sundays in October, haunted golf (complete with people coming out of the bushes and scary music). (Open daily noon-9p, March to October.)

PAINTBALL

LEHIGH VALLEY PAINTBALL

11 MIN *405 S. 5th St., Emmaus*
610-965-0377
www.lehighvalleypaintball.com

POCONO MOUNTAIN PAINTBALL

34 MIN *Nesquehoning*
800-876-0285
www.playpaintballhere.com

SKIRMISH USA

33 MIN *Jim Thorpe*
800-SKIRMISH
www.skirmish.com

RAFTING & CANOEING

JIM THORPE RIVER ADVENTURES

33 MIN *Jim Thorpe*
800-424-RAFT
www.jtraft.com

LEHIGH RIVER WATER TRAIL

wildlandspa.org/lrwt

POCONO WHITEWATER ADVENTURES

33 MIN *Jim Thorpe*
800-WHITEWATER
www.whitewaterrafting.com

ROLLER SKATING

SKATEAWAY ROLLER RINK

12 MIN *Lehigh St. & MacArthur Rd., Whitehall*
610-432-5002

SKATEBOARDING

PENNSKATE

10 MIN *1000 MacArthur Rd., Whitehall*
610-437-2452
www.pennskate.com

SKIING & WINTERSPORTS

TERRY HILL WINTER & WATER PARKS

17 MIN *1000 Hamilton Blvd., Breinigsville*
610-395-0222
www.terryhill.com

Terry Hill Winter Park is best known for its snow-tubing. Drop down an 80-foot run that includes three moguls for an intense wintertime thrill. The park boasts 100 percent man-made snow and offers an exciting adventure for guests of all ages. You're never too old for an exhilarating trip down a snowy hill upon an inflatable inner tube. The Terry Hill Water Park is just as fun, only now there's sun and water slides to bring out your inner child. It claims to be "what a water park should be" with pools and slides all within a safe, friendly, family-oriented atmosphere. The park also offers reservations and catering for picnics, reunions and receptions. Average price for entry is $16 per person. (Opening hours are seasonal; call ahead.)

BEAR CREEK SKI RESORT

21 MIN *101 Doe Mountain Ln., Macungie*
800-233-4131
www.skibearcreek.com

OUT&ABOUT

BLUE MOUNTAIN SKI AREA

28 *1660 Blue Mountain Dr., Palmerton*
MIN 610-826-7700
www.skibluemt.com

CAMELBACK SKI AREA

54 *Camelback Rd., Tannersville*
800-233-8100
MIN www.skicamelback.com

PENNSYLVANIA SKI AREA ASSOCIATION

www.skipa.com

THEME PARKS

DORNEY PARK & WILDWATER KINGDOM

4 *3830 Dorney Park Rd.*
610-395-3724
MIN www.dorneypark.com

Looking for some "thrills and spills" within minutes from campus? Originally a trout fishing getaway established before the Civil War, Dorney Park (& Wildwater Kingdom)— as the ad screams—now offer "two great parks for the price of one!" With eight roller coasters, Dorney Park has enough to keep most thrill-seekers happy. Talon is the tallest and longest inverted roller coaster in the Northeast, and Steel Force was the first coaster in the East to reach heights over 205 feet. (But who's counting?) The newest addition, Hydra: The Revenge, opened in May 2007. This floorless coaster will yank riders through seven inversions, a zero gravity "experience," and several drops below ground level. If you're afraid of heights or ludicrous speed, try out Dorney Park's other, closer-to-the-ground rides, or arcades, games, live shows and shopping. When it's hot, cool off at the Wildwater Kingdom:

wave pools, body slides, tube slides and a lazy river. Grab a few friends and a float and hit Aquablast—one of the longest elevated slides in the world. Prices fluctuate depending on the season, time of day, and group size; bargain hunters should wait for the cheaper autumn evening rates. (Opening hours vary wildly; check the website for details.)

EVERYTHING ELSE

BALLOONATICS AND AERONUTS

29 *7 Harmony-Brass Castle Rd., Phillipsburg NJ*
MIN 877-4 FUN FLY
www.areonuts.com

Attention all sightseers and thrill-seekers. Phillipsburg's own Balloonatics and Aeronauts is sure to get your heart racing and your eyes bulging, all at a couple hundred feet. Pilot Fred Grotenhuis—a 30-plus year veteran—hosts your sunrise or afternoon hot air balloon flight. You'll be airborne for about an hour, but leave at least three for your "flying adventure," which ends with a champagne picnic. Yet if the fun seems endless, so are the precautions and preliminary requirements, so be sure to start planning your outing far in advance. (Reservations are required.) The prices are as high as the hot air balloons, but group rates (and gift certificates) make it more affordable. So stand strong in the face of vertigo, dress comfortably, and start flying high.

THE DAVINCI SCIENCE CENTER

4 *3145 Hamilton Blvd.*
484-664-1002
MIN www.davinci-center.org

Think way back when, probably on or about 5th grade when you may have made that memorable field trip to the Liberty Science Center—memorable then, maybe, but now, no chance. This similar science sanctuary, equipped with hands-on exhibit stations with topics relating to patient care, living things, and meteorology, really gets those youngsters minds flowing, but not ours. It's a great place for elementary school kids, teachers, and field trips (when you're in elementary school). Maybe you could recommend it to your little nephew or niece who happens to live near or around the Lehigh Valley area. Otherwise, you might want to skip this one. (Open M-Sa 9:30a-5p; Su noon-5p.)

THE DOWNS AT LEHIGH VALLEY

14 *1780 Airport Rd.*
610-266-6559
MIN www.pnotw.com/lehi.shtml

Off-track betting at its most depressing. We love it!

EDGEWOOD VALLEY FARMS BULL MADNESS RODEOS

35 *106 Edgewood Ln., Nazareth*
610-759-3340
MIN www.edgewoodvalleyfarms.com

It's a taste of the West right in our own back yard. During the summer months, Edgewood Valley Farms operates its own real-live rodeo on Saturday nights. For $12, you can enjoy a night full of bull-riding, barrel-racing, and chute-dogging. Make sure to bring your own blankets and chairs for optimal seating, and don't forget a cowboy hat if you want to blend in with the crowd. (Open Sa 7:30a-10p in the summer.)

LEHIGH VALLEY SPORTING CLAYS

16 *2750 Limestone St., Coplay*
610-261-9616
MIN www.lvsclays.com

Frustrated with classes? Don't take it out on your roommate. Shoot clays instead! If you're new to sporting clays, there are trained instructors who provide us blue-staters with free instruction. The 120 acres of 5-stand and 17-station courses are set in a beautiful mix of woods, water-filled quarries, old buildings, and fields. (Open W-Su 9:30a-5p.)

OUT&ABOUT

EXCURSIONS

DAY TRIPS

HISTORIC BETHLEHEM

17 MIN *Main St., Bethlehem*
610-868-1513
www.bethlehem.info

When picturing a "downtown," charming rows of historical buildings with candle-lit windows don't typically come to mind. But that's just what you'll find in historic Bethlehem. A mix of storefronts, offices and Moravian Church buildings transport visitors back 250 years—with plenty of up-to-date restaurants (try the popular Bethlehem Brew Works (see page 50) or the nearby Apollo Grill), boutiques and antique shops. It's also a real-life example of urban revitalization (and a good lesson for other cities): Bethlehem officials and citizens successfully reinvented this once run-down area into one of the most highly trampled streets in the Lehigh Valley. Try and time your next trip during a weekend fair (in the spring and fall) or summer's MusikFest (see page 67). The city's Southside is younger and edgier, with bars, galleries, tattoo parlors and the Banana Factory (see page 73)—all crowded between the Lehigh River, the derelict Bethlehem Steel Works and the steep-sloped Lehigh University.

JIM THORPE

33 MIN *Jim Thorpe*
www.jimthorpe.com

Jim Thorpe, born Mauch Chunk but renamed for the great Olympian in a 1954 publicity stunt, bursts into fiery life in the fall. Tucked in a steep Pocono valley along a sharp bend in the Lehigh River, Jim Thorpe's breathtaking forest-peak beauty encircles a stately Victorian village—the setting for the 1970s classic *The Molly Maguires*. Jim Thorpe's mines closed down decades ago, sending the once booming coal town into a tailspin, but adventure-seeking tourists have long since replaced the grimy hands. Shops, B&Bs, galleries, swanky restaurants—even a restored opera house!—crowd its meandering, sloped streets. Before heading for the hills, be sure to tour the regal Asa Packer Mansion, a monument to Victorian excess once home to the fabulously wealthy coal magnate. But head for the hills you must: For all its gabled charm, Jim Thorpe's real draw is its stunning surroundings, with abundant hiking, biking, fishing, river rafting (see page 85), and even paintballing (see page 85). Take the narrow-gauge, aptly named Switchback Railroad up a steep slope for panoramic views of the mountain-squeezed village. (You'll understand why the town has earned its nickname, "The Switzerland of America.")

LEHIGH VALLEY WINE TRAIL

www.lehighvalleywinetrail.com

Here's another trail to add to Pennsylvania's long list of them...but this one's got treats! The Lehigh Valley Wine Trail promotes eight local family-owned wineries and organizes special events—like the Nouveau Weekend in late November, which celebrates the new harvest, and March Madness, a more refined all-day wine binge. While not quite like touring the famed Napa Valley or France's Bourdeaux, this trail is an excellent, upscale (but inexpensive) weekend outing. After sampling a glass or two (or three or four...), you'll feel like you're in California or France anyway. Cheers!

NEW HOPE

64 *New Hope*
MIN www.newhopepa.com

With everything from old-fashioned country crafts to live entertainment and the occasional sex shop, the Village of New Hope is a perfect weekend fieldtrip no matter what you're in the mood for. History buffs can tour a number of historical sites near "Washington's Crossing" (where George traversed the Delaware River during the Revolutionary War). Carriage rides, ferry trips and walking tours are other ways to see the area. And there are more than enough opportunities to blow some cash on four main streets and cobblestone side-streets—in galleries, antique shops and boutiques. For some culture, this artistic hub has the Bucks County Play House (student tickets are just $20) as well as drag shows, and an eclectic mix of cabaret, jazz and retro music. Whatever you do, you're bound to work up an appetite; satisfy your cravings in a casual spot or one of the fancier restaurants overlooking the river.

SHORT-TERM

BEAR JUNCTION CORN MAZE

27 *Rte. 309 & Mountain Rd., New Tripoli*
MIN 610-298-8887
www.bearrockjunction.com

This *four-mile-wide* corn maze, Pennsylvania's largest, challenges visitors through twists and turns and into many dead-ends. Fear not: Numbered checkpoints along the way let you know that you're headed in the right direction. You can carbo-load

before venturing into the maze (in case it takes a while), or refuel when you return (in case it took a while) at the snack bar (which also serves lunch and dinner). Or purchase a s'mores kit and roast marshmallows right on-site. There's also a Farmer's Market, as well as activities—from pumpkin launching to tricycle racing—for the younger crowd. Haunted Nights (Fridays and Saturdays in October) are another great way to gear up for Halloween. (Open Sept.-Nov. Th-Su; call for specific hours.)

THE CRAYOLA FACTORY

25 *30 Center Sq., Easton*
MIN 610-515-8000
www.crayola.com/factory

Don't let the name fool you: The Crayola Factory isn't a factory at all. It's an excuse to let kids run wild and drain every last drop of their creative juices. The Factory occupies a brand-new building in Easton's lovely Center Square. Downstairs, though, is a *canal museum*—the actual Crayola "Factory" is up the stairs. At one station, guests observe how Crayola products are made—hence the "Factory," we suppose. But the rest of the place is dedicated to kids, young kids, who get to test the latest Crayola products—which are conveniently on sale in the gift shop. To appreciate the place, you must be in touch with your inner child—to the point of battling it out for all the good crayons at the craft stations. Otherwise, wait until you have kids of your own. The best thing about the Factory, it turns out, is the drive to Easton, with its sweeping views of the Lehigh Valley and the mountains that cradle it. Why not just take the drive, and save yourself nine bucks?

OUT&ABOUT

CRYSTAL CAVE

29 *963 Crystal Cave Rd.,*
Kutztown
MIN 610-683-6765
www.crystalcavepa.com

In the mood for some quality time in Pennsylvania's wide-open spaces? Or maybe a little miniature golf? Then the Crystal Cave is just what the doctor ordered. And that's only what's above ground. The highlight of a visit is (at least) six feet under—caves that sparkle thanks to calcium crystals that nature's been working on for centuries. Guided tours run daily and have drawn millions since the caverns were discovered in 1871. So delve deep! (Opening hours vary seasonally; call for details.)

LEHIGH VALLEY ZOO

22 *5150 Game Preserve Rd.,*
Shnecksville
MIN 610-799-4171
www.lvzoo.org

Unleash your inner animal and head to the Lehigh Valley Zoo. The setting is more exciting than the animals, as the zoo is up on a plateau in the middle of the sprawling Trexler Game Preserve. With its 1200 acres, the zoo is no small barn, but of course don't go expecting the Bronx Zoo. Then again, it only costs $5.50. No lions, tigers or bears, but you may spy otters, wolves, kangaroos, elk, camels, ostriches, and lots and lots of bison. (Open April-October daily 9:30a-5p.)

LOST RIVER CAVERNS

21 *Durham St., Hellertown*
610-838-8767
MIN www.lostcave.com

Stalagmites and stalactites galore—but, thankfully, no bats—fill a five-chambered cave (accidentally discovered by a limestone quarrying crew in 1883) below Hellertown. Named after the mysterious "Lost River" (whose source is unknown) that flows through them, the caverns were made visitor-friendly thanks to handrails and lighting added in 1930. The crystal formations, fluorescent minerals and crystal-clear underground waterway are an incredible sight to see. But even if all that nature doesn't grab you, the Caverns' sordid history might: Bootleggers hid contraband alcohol here during Prohibition. More recently, it's been a frequent pick for fraternity initiation ceremonies and the backdrop for over 80 weddings. If you go, bring a jacket (it's always a cool 52 degrees underground) and don't miss the gift shop (where you can design your own stone jewelry).

MACK TRUCK FACTORY TOUR

13 *997 Postal Rd.*
610-709-3566
MIN www.macktrucks.com/
default.aspx?pageid=45

We're pretty sure you've never done anything like this—a factory tour on heavy-duty truck assembly. While the tours are free of charge, they are few and far between, and only on Tuesdays and Fridays. Safety comes first, so be prepared to sport appropriate footwear and safety goggles. A minimum group size of five people and a reservation are essential. If you're on the lookout for a unique day trip, round up a group of friends and pile into the bed of your pickup to prepare for this truly country experience. (Reserved tours Tu & F 8a-1p.)

MARTIN GUITAR FACTORY

26 *510 Sycamore St., Nazareth*
610-759-2837
MIN www.martinguitar.com/visit/
tour.html

The phrase "all-in-one" comes to mind when visiting the Martin Guitar Factory. For the music (especially guitar) enthusiast, this tour is informative and enthralling: You get to watch the guitar- and string-making process on some of the finest crafted instruments in the world. For the rest of us, the tour may not be worth it, though the "1833 Shop" (aka gift shop) deserves its own visit. (Tours M-F at 1p; 1833 Shop open M-F 8:30a-5p.) Not far from the factory is the Guitarmaker's Connection, 10 W. North St., in the old Martin factory building. This acoustic guitar supply shop stocks everything from tone woods, kits, parts, tools, glues, tuning machines, finishing supplies, pickups, amps, mics, instrument construction and repair books, and any other accessory you could ever possibly need for your guitar. (Open M-F 9a-4p.)

NO. 9 MINE & MUSEUM

55 *8 Dock Street, Lansford*
570-645-7074
MIN no9mine.tripod.com

In the mood to ride by rail into a mine or experience first-hand the adventures of a coal miner? Then look no further than the No. 9 Mine & Museum. Descend into the bowels of one of America's oldest coal mines. (Tours run May through October.)

PEZ DISPENSER MUSEUM

25 *15-19 S. Bank St., Easton*
888-THE-PEZ1
MIN www.eastonmuseumofpez.com

Though Muhlenberg students are familiar with the Haas College Center—

named for the fourth president of the College—they may not know the other Haas: Eduard Haas III, who invented PEZ candy in 1927 in Vienna. Twenty years later, he developed the PEZ dispenser, enabling the citizens of over 60 countries to have their PEZ and eat it too. This now-popular kid's collectible was originally produced for adult smokers in Austria before migrating to the U.S. in the fifties. The first dispenser looked like cigarette lighters, on the assumption that the compressed peppermint breath mints might be used to curb smokers' addictions. After researchers realized the dispensers' appeal to kids and collectors, PEZ was redesigned to feature the fruity flavors and loveable candy popping heads we know today. In 2003, Kevin and Tim Coyle decided to pay tribute to this invention by opening the third PEZ museum in the country. Located in nearby Easton, the PEZ Dispenser Museum displays over 1500 dispensers in creative settings. You can see Disney dispensers housed in a ten-foot high castle or the members of the Beatles on their own stage. After scanning the display of 500 dispensers to discover "Where's Waldo?," you can move on to the gift shop that sells hundreds of PEZ products—all for $5. (Curb your PEZ addiction Tu-Su 10a-5p.)

STRAWBERRY ACRES

19 *5120 Overlook Rd., Coplay*
610-261-2323
MIN www.strawberryacres.com

A pick-your-own fruit farm, from apples to pumpkins to raspberries.

OUT&ABOUT

WEYERBACHER BREWING COMPANY

30 *905G Line St., Easton*
MIN 610-559-5561
www.weyerbacher.com

You won't find any Bud at the Weyerbacher Brewing Company. No, just Merry Monks' Ale and Blithering Idiot Barley Wine, among 13 other unconventional brews. That's reason enough to make the trip to Easton for a tour in and around the towering distillers and fermenters. And then there are the free samples: The Blithering Idiot—which, according to the brewery, should be enjoyed in a "brandy snifter or wine glass, preferably in front of the fire or accompanying a literary class"—is 11 percent alcohol. After the tour, you can assemble your own variety case, or even purchase a "Growler"—a one-half gallon jug waiting to be filled with your favorite. Who needs Natty Light? (Open for tours Sa noon-3pm.)

OUT&ABOUT

HISTORY

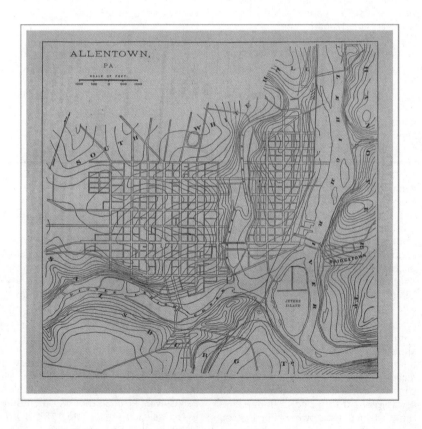

ALLENTOWN,
PA

SCALE OF FEET.
1000 500 0 500 1000

The Lehigh Valley wasn't always coke and steel. Long before Carbondale and Ironton got settled, a prominent colonial jurist named William Allen selected the bluff above the confluence of the Lehigh River and Jordan Creek as the site for his new town. The year was 1762.

The plateau had been an Indian hunting ground. ("Lehigh" itself is an anglicization of the Indian *Lechawaxen,* which roughly translates to "free to roam." Ironies abound.) Ever since England's Charles II "deeded" the future state to the Penn family in the 17th century, the Native American claim to this corner of the "New World" was—to use a euphemism—disputed. One particularly loathsome footnote to the whole land heist happened here, around what would become Allentown.

In 1737, a couple of decades before Allen's town-hunting expedition, William Penn's sons decided that the lands to the north of Philadelphia should be opened for settlement. Their scheme to convince area Indians—the Lenni Lenape—gets remembered as the "Walking Purchase." Here's why: The Penn brothers found an old treaty giving settlers the land "as far as a man can walk in a day and a half." The brothers hired, for their "walk," famous athletes who "walked hard"—hard enough to reach all the way to the peak of the Blue Mountain, the northern boundary of what we now know as the Lehigh Valley.

As recently as 1962, in a volume to commemorate the city's 200-year anniversary, the land grab was still being blamed on Native American naiveté: "The Indian had a feeling for common ownership of all the land, and it was very hard for him to understand the idea of private ownership. In fact, this was one of the basic problems which plagued the red men in their relations with the white man."

William Allen, then Pennsylvania's Chief Justice, named his brand-new village Northampton Town. ("Allentown" wasn't formally adopted until 1838.) In 1767, Allen gave his son James the town and the land around it as a wedding gift, and the younger Allen soon built a hunting lodge "retreat" on a height overlooking the Jordan, known as Trout Hall. (This same Trout Hall was sold, in 1848, to the Allentown Seminary, the institutional precursor to Muhlenberg College. The College was housed on these grounds until it relocated to the current West End campus, in 1904.)

Allentonians seem especially proud of the Liberty Bell's brief Revolutionary War stopover, sheltered here from the British—though James Allen himself was suspected of Tory sympathies.

Where the swift Jordan rushed and rolled
In its never-ending race,
Where the leaves cast shadowy lace,
And the trout were big and bold,
The Lechawaxen loved to roam
Through his mountains, forest-clad

The lines come from "An Ode to Allentown," a tribute in verse to the city's Revolutionary role, published on that 1962 anniversary. The poem is 294 lines long. Like other cities, Allentown's memory is more than a little airbrushed.

For much of its history, Allentown was overshadowed by its Moravian neighbor, Bethlehem. Both cities were mainly settled by Germans—the fabled Pennsylvania Dutch, though Dutch only in the *deutsch* sense. One 1783 visitor from Germany reported that Allentonians "are mainly German who speak bad English and distressing German."

Successive waves of other European immigrants would join the PA Dutch, especially in the early 20th century. But Allentown was still distinctively German enough that a 1939 guide to the state, published by the New Deal Writers Program, described the city as "peopled largely by Pennsylvania Germans." Citing ground hog rituals and barnside hexes, the guide claimed that residents "cling as tenaciously to their old traditions as to their curious but expressive idiom."

Allentown might have remained "Allen's Little Town" were it not for the discovery, in 1792, of coal and iron ore in the mountains to the north—though there wasn't much mining until the 46-mile Lehigh Canal was linked to the Delaware River in 1838. Less than twenty years later, one and a quarter *million* tons of anthracite coal were barged past Allentown and on to Philadelphia every year. And thanks to abundant limestone and sand, a cement industry rapidly formed in the second half of the 19th century. The Lehigh Valley became—is this an honor?—the cement capital of the world.

Allentown was the region's retail and banking center, though it also housed factories of its own. For a few decades the city boasted a thriving silk industry, second only to New Jersey's Paterson. (The beautiful and underused Adelaide Silk Mill, at 3rd and Hamilton, is a hulking monument to all that fabric.)

Businesses with names like the Lehigh Portland Cement Company and the Lehigh Structural Steel Company were headquartered here—and made fortunes for the Trexlers and Traylors in the early decades of the 20th

century. Trexler and the other industrialists ran the city, for better or worse. On the eve of the Depression, the Chamber of Commerce boasted, in its promotional literature, that Allentown is "singularly free from disturbances of any kind."

All the new industry in and around Allentown attracted thousands of immigrants in these years, especially Slavs and Eastern European Jews. Syrians, too, were settling here—most from Syria's Christian Valley, where Pennsylvania German missionaries had thumped Bibles decades before. (Allentown's Syrian community remains vibrant, one of the largest in the world outside Syria.)

When Mack Trucks moved its headquarters here in the 1960s, the city had been booming for decades. Why not the decades to come, too? A 1965 pamphlet, prepared for relocating Mack employees, captured the city's Jetsons-like optimism for the future: "Large passenger-carrying rockets are a definite possibility in the not too distant future..."

American cities didn't know what was coming. Post-war Levittowns and acres of three-bedroom ranches; the interstates and cheap Chevy's; mortgage tax breaks and *Leave it to Beaver*. Cities never had a chance.

It is a uniquely American barbarism that schools and social services get funded through local property tax. In the years after World War II, in Allentown and elsewhere, the white and wealthy got up and left—pooled their resources in the self-segregated enclaves we call suburbs. Cities were left with fewer resources and more burdens, with the working poor, in effect, bankrolling services for the truly poor. Higher taxes *and* under-funded

HISTORY

A 1879 birds-eye-view map of Allentown (Library of Congress)

schools set off a vicious cycle: More flight, more burdens, a weaker tax base, deteriorating schools, more flight, and so on. Call it the soft bigotry of low home values.

Pennsylvania's notoriously weak land use laws made things worse. (The laws are still feeble today, and the Valley's horizon-conquering clusters of cardboard McMansions are the predictable result.)

It didn't help that most, including Allentown, inflicted their own wounds in the form of "urban renewal." Whole blocks in and near downtown were torn down to make room for "some beautiful new structures" (their words, not ours)—brutalist concrete squatheaps. Historic buildings were also razed for parking lots, in a doomed bid to compete with the Lehigh Valley Mall, which opened in 1976 on land—here's a bitter irony—sold by the city and annexed to Whitehall Township.

And then there was deindustrialization. From the 60s onward, the U.S.—and Northeastern cities in particular—were hemorrhaging manufacturing jobs. Bethlehem Steel, symbol of Valley industry, laid off 2,500 employees on "Black Friday" in 1977; the company would limp along for nearly two decades. Its flagship Bethlehem plant closed in 1995.

Allentown, like most cities in the postwar era, was under assault on multiple fronts. We often talk about cities as if they are people, down-on-their-luck sorts who can't get back on their feet. But the decline of U.S. cities—Philadelphia and Detroit, Reading and York, Hartford and Lowell—had nothing to do with luck. That decline had everything to do with policy—with conscious choices about transportation dollars, school funding and tax writeoffs. Our abandoned cities stand, given these choices, as an indictment in brick and mortar.

Allentown eluded the fate of so many of its municipal peers, for a very long time. By some measures, it has even made *headway* against a strong current: The city's population is larger today than it was in 1950, in contrast to every other Pennsylvanian city. (Philadelphia, for example, has lost over 900,000 residents, or close to 40 percent of its population!) Allentown's downtown residential neighborhoods remain healthy. Crime rates and vacancy are strikingly low.

But decline *did* happen here, only later and more suddenly than in other cities. And it happened on Hamilton Street, for so long the region's retail hub, in a very visible way: Hess's and Leh's, the legendary department stores downtown, closed within a year of one another, in 1996. A sinkhole destroyed the brand-new, glass-and-steel Corporate Center at 7th and Hamilton, in 1997. Within a single decade, the city's once bejeweled main street was largely emptied out. No wonder Bob Wittman, longtime journalist, titled essays on these years, "Bad Luck, Bad Times: Allentown 1993-1995" and "Ground Zero: Allentown 1995-1997."

Much of this was symbolic—a sinkhole had swallowed the city's flagship office building, after all—but all the more traumatic as a result. Native Allentonians, when you meet them, often come off as shell-shocked. The Hess's closing, in particular, has left a deep psychological scar, and always gets mentioned in "the city's gone to hell" declarations that newcomers routinely receive.

There's often a racist edge to these rants. The city's large Puerto Rican population is singled out, through innuendo and blunt accusation, as the cause of the decline. (In 1994, *The New York Times Magazine* ran a cover story on "The Latinization of Allentown.")

The claim is absurd, as the steady migration of Puerto Rican residents *saved* the city from an almost certain population plunge. One of the depressing ironies is that Allentown has hosted a thriving Puerto Rican community since the 1950s, as Muhlenberg historian Anna Adams reminds us in her *Hidden From History*.

The city's Latinos—Puerto Ricans, yes, but also Dominicans, Mexicans, Cubans, Salvadorans and others—now comprise about a quarter of the city's residents. And they *have* changed the face of the city. For the better: Allentown's downtown neighborhoods are healthy and alive as a result.

Traumatized and occasionally racist, many native Allentonians have waged a relentless whisper campaign against the city. Allentown-bashing is the stuff of countless private conversations, passed along from real estate agent to plumber to professor. New residents are marinated in this kind of talk.

The Allentown of the "whisper campaign" doesn't look like the Allentown *we* saw. But it's worrying all the same: There's something self-fulfilling about all the acidic self-description. A city's fate, in large part, hinges on perception. Today's talk—however distorted now—is tomorrow's reality. Hear "Don't go downtown; it's unsafe" enough and no one will go downtown. And then it *will* be unsafe.